Words of Wisdom for Women at the Well

QUENCHING YOUR HEART'S THIRST FOR LOVE AND INTIMACY

WORDS OF WISDOM FOR

WOMEN
at the WELL

*Q*uenching Your Heart's Thirst
for Love and Intimacy

SHANNON ETHRIDGE

Essence
PUBLISHING

Belleville, Ontario, Canada

All Scripture quotations, unless otherwise specified, are from *Disciple's Study Bible*, New International Version, (Nashville, TN: Holman Bible Publishers, 1984).

National Library of Canada Cataloguing in Publication
Ethridge, Shannon
    Words of wisdom for women at the well : quenching your heart's thirst for love and intimacy / Shannon Ethridge.
Includes bibliographical references.
ISBN 1-55306-676-6.--ISBN 1-55306-678-2 (LSI ed.)

    1. Christian women--Religious life. 2. Women-- Conduct of life.
I. Title.
BV4527.E74 2003   248.8'43   C2003-904356-8

Essence Publishing is a Christian Book Publisher dedicated to furthering the work of Christ through the written word. For more information, contact:
20 Hanna Court, Belleville, Ontario, Canada K8P 5J2.
Phone: 1-800-238-6376 • Fax: (613) 962-3055.
E-mail: publishing@essencegroup.com
Internet: www.essencegroup.com

Printed in Canada
by

Essence
PUBLISHING

Are You a Woman at the Well?

___ ___   1. Is having a man in your life or finding a husband something that dominates your thoughts?

___ ___   2. Are you ever accused by friends of being flirtatious?

___ ___   3. Have you made promises to yourself about avoiding a particular person or act, only to find yourself breaking that promise?

___ ___   4. Does the word "codependent" describe you at all?

___ ___   5. Do you have sexual secrets you wouldn't want anyone to know about?

___ ___   6. Do you feel like a nobody if you do not have a love interest in your life? Does a romantic relationship give you a sense of identity?

___ ___   7. Have you had sex at inappropriate times, in inappropriate places, or with inappropriate people (i.e., someone you are not currently married to)?

___ ___   8. Have you found yourself in compromising positions in relationships?

___ ___   9. Have you ever teased or flirted with someone until he called your bluff or confronted you?

___ ___   10. Do you keep a list in your head of how many sexual partners or boyfriends you have had?

___ ___   11. Have you lost count of partners or boyfriends?

___ ___   12. Have you had sex even though you knew you could get a disease or become pregnant?

___ ___   13. Do you seem to attract bad relationships or dysfunctional men (or women)?

_____ _____ 14. Do you feel that men would not want to be with you unless you were willing to have sex?

_____ _____ 15. Are you bored unless you have someone to flirt with?

_____ _____ 16. Does the song, "Looking For Love In All The Wrong Places" strike a chord in you?

_____ _____ 17. Have you had your reputation damaged by relationships?

_____ _____ 18. Is remaining faithful to one person on a long-term basis challenging for you?

_____ _____ 19. If God called you to remain single the rest of your life, would you be dissatisfied?

_____ _____ 20. Have you ever used sex or relationships to "medicate" your emotional pain?

_____ _____ 21. Are you unable to concentrate on work, school, or your household because of thoughts or feelings you are having about someone else?

_____ _____ 22. When you look in the mirror, do you dislike or disrespect the person you see?

_____ _____ 23. Do you feel as if you are unclean, undignified, used, or broken?

_____ _____ 24. Does your sex or love life affect your spiritual life in a negative way?

_____ _____ 25. Do you feel that there is more that God could do with your life if you were not distracted by sexual or romantic pursuits?

There is no "magic number" that will determine if you are in need of healing in this area, but if reading through these questions has brought home to you the fact that your sexual activity, romantic behavior, or emotional involvements are a hindrance to your spiritual growth, then let's go to the well together where Jesus awaits us with Living Water!

Table of Contents

Preface

Since the early days of playing house and dressing Barbie dolls, little girls have been wishing... wishing for Daddy to come home... wishing we could be the center of attention... wishing for someone to hold our hand, look into our eyes and tell us how precious we are.

As blossoming young women, our wishing turned toward being rescued from the other wallflowers and then escorted onto the dance floor... wishing for true love's first kiss... wishing to wear the coveted senior ring.

As adults, our patterns of wishful thinking have often continued... wishing for our knight in shining armor to gallop into town... wishing for our Prince Charming to come and sweep us off our feet... wishing to hear those three magic words whispered into our ear. Or perhaps your wishes have turned to the past rather than the future... wishing you could forget yesterday's many abuses or regrets... wishing the husband you now have was more attentive or exciting... wishing that you had held out for someone or something better in life.

Unfortunately, many women have wished so long and so hard for relational satisfaction in their lives that they have "wished" themselves into many a predicament. Jesus met such a woman at a well once. She had a string of broken relationships behind her. She didn't know how to exist without a man by her side. She was bound by chains of sexual immorality. She was living with a man that was not her husband, and her future only promised continued disillusionment. That is, until Jesus came to visit that Woman at the Well.

[Jesus] *came to a town in Samaria called Sychar, near the plot of ground Jacob had given to his son Joseph. Jacob's well was there, and Jesus, tired as He was from the journey, sat down by the well. It was about the sixth hour.*

When a Samaritan woman came to draw water, Jesus said to her, "Will you give me a drink?" (His disciples had gone into the town to buy food.)

The Samaritan woman came to Him, "You are a Jew and I am a Samaritan woman. How can you ask me for a drink?" (For Jews do not associate with Samaritans.)

Jesus answered her, "If you knew the gift of God and who it is that asks you for a drink, you would have asked Him and He would have given you living water."

"Sir," the woman said, "you have nothing to draw with and the well is deep. Where can you get this living water? Are you greater than our father Jacob, who gave us the well and drank from it himself, as did also his sons and his flocks and herds?"

Jesus answered, "Everyone who drinks this water will be thirsty again, but whoever drinks the water I give [her] will never thirst. Indeed, the water I give [her] will become in [her] a spring of water welling up to eternal life."

The woman said to Him, "Sir give me this water so that I won't get thirsty and have to keep coming here to draw water."

He told her, "Go, call your husband and come back."

"I have no husband," she replied.

Jesus said to her, "You are right when you say you have no husband. What you have just said is quite true."

"Sir," the woman said, "I can see that you are a prophet. Our fathers worshiped on this mountain, but you Jews claim that the place where we must worship is in Jerusalem."

Jesus declared, "Believe me, woman, a time is coming when you will worship the Father neither on this mountain nor in Jerusalem. You Samaritans worship what you do not know; we worship what we do know, for salvation is from the Jews. Yet a time is coming and has now come when the true worshippers will worship the Father in spirit and truth, for they are the kind of worshippers the Father seeks. God is spirit, and His worshippers must worship in spirit and in truth."

The woman said, "I know that Messiah" (called Christ) "is coming. When He comes, He will explain everything to us."

Then Jesus declared, "I who speak to you am He" (John 4:4–26).

I find it interesting that Jesus did not bother to question this woman as to why she was having an affair. He did not ask her what happened in her childhood that would justify her immoral actions. He did not ask her what kind of pain she was trying to escape through her relational involvements. Jesus obviously knew it would do no good to allow this woman an opportunity to "blame" her sin on external factors, as is a common response in today's society to dysfunctional behaviors. (We'll talk about the "blame pit" later!)

No, Jesus masterfully cut right to the chase. He knew she was looking for love in all the wrong places. He knew He was the only one who could provide the love that continued to elude her, relationship after relationship. He knew she was thirsty for something real. He knew that she had been drinking "stagnant water," and only He could quench the thirst in her spirit. He wanted to satisfy her in a way no other man possibly could. He offered her a drink of "Living Water," so that her very soul itself would know complete satisfaction for the first time.

The good news for us is that Jesus Christ is the same yesterday, today, and forever (Hebrews 13:8). He still stands at the well, awaiting broken women to approach Him with parched lips and dry throats, desperate for something to satisfy their weary souls. My sisters, have you ever wondered what it would be like to have the thirst of your soul quenched in such a way that you would never thirst again? In your desperate attempts to find someone to love you, are you aware that Jesus Christ longs to be the Lover of your Soul? Are you aware that there is a new life waiting for you that is free from the stresses, worries, dangers, and emotional roller-coaster rides of inappropriate relational involvements? We serve a God who longs to see you at peace in your relationship with Him, who longs to fill you with all of the fruits of His Spirit—love, joy, peace, patience, kindness, goodness, gentleness [and most of all, what Women at the Well seem to lack most]—*faithfulness* and *self-control* (Galatians 5:22–23a).

Before we begin our journey away from "stagnant water" (earthly relationships) and toward "Living Water" (a heavenly affair), I want to acknowledge that it took great strength for you to look inside yourself and to honestly answer the "Are You a Woman at the Well?" questionnaire. You may feel a sense of desperation over recognizing your need for healing in this area of your life, but do not let that overwhelming feeling cloud the fact that you already have the biggest of victories behind you. Recognizing that you struggle with this issue is half of the battle. When the Holy Spirit brings conviction, it is because He is ready to bring change.

God wants to transform you from a *Woman at the Well* into a *Well Woman*. Just like the Samaritan woman experienced centuries ago, a face-to-face encounter with Jesus Christ heals your wounds and satisfies your thirst for a genuinely fulfilling relationship. Such an encounter can bring years of dysfunctional patterns to a close and help you begin living a life of virtue. You may be thinking, "Who? Me? I'm not exactly the virtuous type!" Ironically, God does not call the equipped; He equips the called. He desires to equip you with dignity, honor, and self-respect, so that you can become the godly woman that He created you to be.

As you begin this journey, remember to be patient. There are no quick fixes or shortcuts to healing. Just as you did not become a Woman at the Well overnight, you will not become a Well Woman overnight. It is a process, but God is faithful to bring to completion (perfection) the good work that He begins in you. Don't be discouraged at the road ahead, thinking that the change is going to be "too difficult to manage." That is a lie from the pit of hell! The truth is that it takes more energy and emotional investment in order to continue seeking "stagnant water," through sexual and romantic pursuits with men, than it does to stop that vicious cycle and allow Jesus Christ to be the Lover of your Soul. Once you taste Living Water, you'll never go back to stagnant water again!

These words of wisdom that we will be examining together are a collection from Scriptures and a variety of different sources (which I have referenced at the back of this book, so that you can enjoy them as much as I have). They are the invaluable jewels and precious tidbits of revelation that God has shown me to pick up along the path of my own journey toward healing. As difficult as this journey has been, I have actually become quite grateful for it.

"*Grateful?*" you say? How can one be "*grateful*" for such an ailment? Well, had I not been so sick, I would have never understood how great a healer God really is. Had I never been so desperate for attention and affection, I would never have discovered the joy of crawling up into my Heavenly Father's lap and listening to Him whisper affirmations into my ear. Had I not been looking so frantically for love, I might have missed the most incredibly intimate moments of my life—those shared with Jesus, the ultimate Lover. This desperation to discover sexual and emotional integrity has certainly been challenging, but it is through this process that I have come to testify, as Paul did in 2 Corinthians 12:9–10:

> *The Lord said to me, 'My grace is sufficient for you, for my power is made perfect in weakness.' Therefore I will boast all the more gladly about my weaknesses, so that Christ's power may rest on me. That is why, for Christ's sake, I delight in weaknesses, in insults, in hardships, in persecutions, in difficulties. For when I am weak, then I am strong.*

Perhaps you are wondering if this kind of transformation is possible for you. The question to ask yourself is not, "Am I strong enough to change?" The question to ask is, "Does God have enough strength to change me?" Your answer to that question reveals more about yourself than it does about God.

At this point, all you really need is faith in God's redemptive power and a willingness to surrender to the mighty work He longs to do in you. Believe that God is ready and capable of transforming you from a *Woman at the Well* into a *Well Woman!*

> *Ask and it will be given to you; seek and you will find; knock and the door will be opened to you. For everyone who asks receives; [she] who seeks finds; and to [her] who knocks, the door will be opened* (Matthew 7:7–8).

CHAPTER ONE

The Neon Sign

*I tell you the truth, unless a kernel of wheat
falls to the ground and dies, it remains only a single seed.
But if it dies, it produces many seeds.*
—JOHN 12:24A

The "guards" were heavily armed and ready to protect the bank from any "bad guys" who might wander in. My four-year-old son, Matthew, stood on one side of the entrance door to the bank lobby with a toy bow and arrow in ready position. On the other side of the door stood his friend Cameron, also four, with an impressive plastic sword drawn from its sheath. As I stood in line at the teller window, I noticed all of the bank patrons looking on appreciatively at these self-appointed guards with a sense of relief that they were in such capable hands.

That is when *she* walked in—a long-legged brunette in high heels, a form-fitting miniskirt and spaghetti-strap top. The young guards glanced at one another and the rest of the onlookers turned their heads, as if watching a tennis match—first eyeballing the woman, then the boys, then the woman again. As this scantily clad bombshell strutted across the bank lobby, made an ATM transaction, and then strutted back out of the armed doors, I sensed that everyone in the lobby was holding their breath and wondering, "What could be going through those boys' minds?"

As soon as the door closed and the woman was out of earshot, Cameron satisfied everyone's curiosity. He leaned over to Matthew and loudly exclaimed, "The Bible *warns* about women like *that!*"

Of course, we all laughed hysterically at the insight that came from the mouth of that babe. My first reaction to this woman was, "Wow, does she have a neon sign on her forehead!"

However, the Holy Spirit quickly humbled me with a reminder that I didn't have a stone to throw. Only a few short years before, I, too, was wearing such a neon sign. How I wished I could have had the opportunity to share my personal testimony with her.

My Own Neon Sign

I was raised in the church, but I was a very rebellious teenage girl and began the search for someone to "love" me at age fourteen. That search led me into a predicament that I was physically unable to get myself out of, and I was date-raped by an eighteen-year-old boy. I felt at the time as if my virginity had been stolen from me, so, in my mind, there was really no reason not to give in to the sexual temptations that dating later offered. I gave in, time after time, creating a list in my mind which would eventually grow too lengthy to recall.

This pattern of looking for love only to have it elude me, relationship after relationship, continued for many years, until I returned to church at age twenty-one. There, I met a wonderful Christian man, and I began working alongside him as a counselor in our church's youth group. I was surprised as we began dating that his concerns about me did not include coercing me into bed. Greg was a twenty-six-year-old virgin who treated me with respect and honor. During our courtship, I tried to explain to him that there had been many sexual partners in my past (assuming he would then change his mind about me), but he interrupted me every time, saying, "I don't care about your past. I only care about your future and I want to be a part of helping you to become all that God created you to be."

What woman wouldn't be faithful to a guy like that, right? Still, my faithfulness to my husband was much more of a struggle than I had ever anticipated. I had been under the impression that putting a wedding band on my finger would totally change me, and I had felt confident that my husband's love would be enough to save me from my own destructive behaviors. However, I soon discovered that, as great a husband as Greg was, a savior he was not (nor should any husband be expected to be).

Although I modified my behavior a great deal, many root issues remained beneath the surface, and many years of emotional baggage were yet to be fully unpacked. I soon discovered that even though I was *married*, I certainly was not *buried!* I was not dead to the temptations that continued to plague me. Satan was a roaring lion seeking to devour me, my marriage, and my ministry. The Sunday-school knowledge I had of God at that time made me oblivious to the fact that only an intimate love affair with Christ would save me from myself and transform me from the woman I had been into the woman I wanted to be.

The Storm Before the Calm

Five years into our marriage, my husband and I had dinner at our friends' house one December evening. I went to bed as soon as we returned home, feeling quite exhausted at this point in the holidays. However, I was wide awake suddenly at two a.m., unsure why I couldn't go back to sleep. I lay there for quite a while, and my thoughts turned to God. I had not been faithful to regular quiet times with Him, so I asked, "Lord, did You wake me up because You wanted to talk with me?"

I heard a soft shower begin outside my window. As I listened to the unexpected rain, I sensed that I was conversing with God through nature (as bizarre as it may sound), so I asked the Lord, "Are You trying to tell me something?" The rain grew stronger and seemed to be saying that *someone was about to die.* I asked, "Lord, is that it? Are You trying to tell me someone is going to die?" The sky grumbled ominously.

I thought, "My grandfather or grandmother! They are in a nursing home and getting feeble. It must be one of them." But I realized that God wouldn't wake me up to tell me to expect something I had already been expecting for years, so I thought, "What if it is one of my parents?" That still didn't seem right in my spirit.

Then I looked over at my snoozing husband and thought, "No, Lord, please do not let it be Greg!" At that time, my biggest fear was that, without my husband alive and holding me accountable, I would most likely return to looking for love in all the wrong places.

My mind next wandered down the hall to my beautiful angel of a daughter in her room, and my gregarious newborn son sleeping soundly in his crib through the storm. With tears streaming down my face, I begged the Lord, "Please! Do *not* let it be someone in this house!" A deafening clap of thunder boomed and a brilliant bolt of lightning illuminated my bedroom, as if God were saying, "Yes, someone *in this house* is about to die."

Drowning in my tears, I wrestled with the Lord in my mind for over two hours. None of my begging seemed to change anything, and I became emotionally drained from panic.

Then the Holy Spirit gave me a gentle reminder of God's promise that He would never give me anything I could not handle. Once I embraced the idea that God would give me whatever strength I needed to endure such a tragic loss, the storm suddenly stopped. No thunder. No lightning. No rain. Just silence. The first sound I heard was the beautiful melody of a chirping bird. Laying there for quite a while longer, thinking that birds never come out and start chirping immediately after a storm, I still could not go back to sleep. I got up and ate a bowl of cereal, and eventually a full tummy helped me return to my slumber.

The next morning, I told my husband every detail of the night's experiences. I asked, "Do you think I was dreaming?"

He turned the question back to me. "Do *you* think you were dreaming?" he said.

I went to the kitchen and saw my empty cereal bowl and spoon in the sink. "No," I replied with worry, "I certainly wasn't dreaming."

The Longest Two Months of My Life

Convinced that someone in my house was in fact about to die, I would not let my husband leave for work each morning without a major production of hugs and kisses. I wanted to make sure that if he died that day, he would die knowing that I loved him. I was hesitant to let either of my children out of my sight. I thought that as long as they were in view, I could keep anything tragic from happening to them.

This nerve-wracking scenario went on for almost two months. I was beginning to crack. Then, one Monday night in mid-February, I went to my Bible Study Fellowship meeting, but couldn't sit with my friends. I slithered into the back pew, alone, with tears of distress staining my cheeks. Silently but desperately, I cried out to the Lord, "I cannot take this limbo any longer! Whoever it is in my house that has to die, Lord, take them! But I can't stand not knowing any more! Go ahead and do what You have to do."

As the teaching leader began her lecture that evening, she had us open our Bibles to John 12:24, "I tell you the truth, unless a kernel of wheat falls to the ground and dies, it remains only a single seed. But if it dies, it produces many seeds."

I could not have heard God more clearly if another lightning bolt had come crashing through the stained glass windows of the church and struck me on the forehead. It was *me* that had to die! I had to die to my *self!*

Although I heard what God said, I left that night not understanding what He meant. Angrily, I muttered at God underneath my breath all the way through the parking lot. "What part of myself have I not died to, God? I wanted to be a doctor, but You wanted me to be a youth minister, so I gave You my vocation! I wanted to spend more money decorating the house, but You asked us to pledge more to our church, so I gave You my finances! I just gave You permission to take your pick of my husband or either one of my children! What more do You want from me? What else is there to die to? I don't know what kind of game You are playing, God, but if there is something that I still need to die to, You are going to have to show me very clearly, because I haven't a clue!"

An Angel in a Tank Top

The very next day I had a noon appointment with a man who taught my aerobics class (I'll call him "James"). What prompted me to accept his lunch invitation was the suspicion that he did not know Jesus. So when he asked me to lunch, I thought that this would be a good opportunity for me to tell him about a loving God who wanted a personal relationship with him. (Yes, many Women at the Well unknowingly use "ministry" as a mask to hide their selfish motives! Had he not been so attractive, and had I not basked in the attention he lavished on me, I am certain I would not have been so concerned with James' soul at the time!)

However, as I was driving to meet him, my prayers were not only for his salvation, but also for my focus to remain on the business at hand. Admittedly, James' bulging biceps were a potential distraction from my mission.

As we sat in the noisy café, I was trying to work up the nerve to put my agenda out on the table and talk to him about God. But

James turned the tables by leaning over into my face and asking, in a low voice, "Do you know why I asked you to lunch today?" Feeling extremely uncomfortable, I responded that I did not.

He whispered, "Because you have a neon sign on your forehead that says that you are hungry for love, attention and affection!"

Fearing that I was being propositioned, I replied, "Well, I am a happily married woman in ministry, so how do I get that neon sign *off* of my forehead?"

James grinned and sincerely responded, "Shannon, you have got to *die* to your *self*."

Was I on Candid Camera? Had this man been a fly on my wall over the past two months? Had he been reading my mail? Or was he a messenger of the Lord in a tank top, confirming what God had told me the night before?

Attempting to gather my wits and hold back the scorching tears that were quickly taking form, I managed to ask, "How *exactly* do I die to myself? I really need to know!"

Just as Jesus spoke the truth in love to the Samaritan woman at the well, James held a mirror to my face that day. I often came to aerobics class dressed not as much to sweat as to cause the men there to sweat! I carried myself more like an attention-seeking missile than a woman on a mission from God. And thankfully, someone finally had the courage to help me see myself as too many others had already seen me—not as a living testimony, but as a walking target.

His Problem or Mine?

I couldn't deny that men rarely treated me with the respect I felt I deserved as a married woman in ministry, a fact that created a very negative impression of men in my mind. I had often wondered, "What is wrong with all these guys who flirt with a girl wearing a wedding ring on her finger? Why would so many men make passes at a woman driving a minivan with a Jesus bumper sticker and an infant seat in the back?"

Never had it occurred to me before that my mannerisms were often teaching, even enticing, men to treat me in such disrespectful ways. "I only dress like other women dress, walk like other girls walk, and talk like others talk," I had reasoned in the past. I had chimed in with many females who claimed, "If a guy can't handle the way I look, that's *his* problem." This attitude *was* a problem—*my* problem!

Once all these things were brought into the light, I couldn't deny that, deep down, I actually enjoyed the excitement of being flirted with and the feeling of power it gave me. No longer could I remain oblivious to the sinful reflection of my soul. This knowledge brought enlightenment and demanded change.

I shared my revelations with my husband later that night. One of the primary saving graces in my marriage has been that I had never hidden anything from my husband, no matter how embarrassing to admit. Before the sun would set each day, he knew my every temptation, my every conversation, my every response, and my every regret. His loving accountability was my life preserver in my struggle to remain emotionally and sexually faithful.

Upon hearing the details of the conversation with James, tears of relief flowed down Greg's cheeks as he explained, "Shannon, I've been praying for five years that someone would come along and help you understand these things about yourself. I have never had the words, but I have known that the Lord would send an angel into your life to reveal these things to you." We both agreed that I should see a Christian female counselor, and my journey toward sexual and emotional restoration began.

Giving God the Wheel

As a Christian, I had always thought that God was in my driver's seat, totally in control of my direction in life. However,

22

through this experience, God showed me how I had often tried to steal the steering wheel away from Him and how dangerous this habit had been. There came a time when I had to give God control of my sexual thoughts and feelings, my temptations and struggles, and my deepest, innermost desires.

Who is in control of your life? Who is in *your* driver's seat? As a Christian, you may think God is. Yet, many of us have created a double life for ourselves, one of which is ruled by Christ and the other of which is ruled by our passions. Our public life shows others that Jesus is our Lord, but our private life is still controlled by our sin nature.

God will not take control over areas we have not yet surrendered to Him. He is a gentleman; He doesn't remove that which has not yet been offered to Him. We may have thought that God was in the driver's seat all these years, but when it comes to our private life, we have managed to steal the steering wheel many times, haven't we?

We must repent from depending on our own abilities to manufacture some resemblance of internal satisfaction. The word "repentance" doesn't mean simply being regretful or remorseful. To repent actually means "to turn and go the opposite direction." We must turn to God and trust in Him to fully satisfy the same unmet needs that have driven us into the arms of other men in the past.

As we learn to lay ourselves on the altar as a living sacrifice to God, we often find the problem with a living sacrifice is that it has a tendency to crawl off of the altar! It seems like we often take two steps forward and one step back. That is okay, as long as we strive to move forward—the race toward wholeness becomes easier as you continue to run toward God!

God Will Prove Himself Daily

You have heard the cliche for years that God can meet all your needs, but have you ever really put Him to the test? He stands ready to prove Himself to you! Be aware of how God works—He is much more concerned with your needs than your wants. You may pray for something you want, but God, who knows what may be coming across your path in the future, is faithful to go beyond your wants to give you what you need. With every new relationship, I used to pray, "Lord, let this one be *the* one!" Then, when "the one" actually did come along, I was so thankful for all of the previously unanswered prayers! God knew what my future held, and His denials were because He was more concerned with what I needed in the long run than with what I wanted at the moment.

Also keep in mind that God does not hand out lifetime supplies of love all in one day. His deepest desire is to have a continuing (daily) personal relationship with you. It is really like being involved in a love affair. Would a phone call from your lover yesterday be enough to satisfy you today? No, you want a daily dose of attention! God wants to give you a daily dose and He wants to receive the same from you. He wants you to be consumed with finding opportunities to rendezvous with Him again and again. Just like He proved Himself to the Israelites in the desert by providing fresh manna each day, God will be faithful to give you exactly what you need to get you through today. And when you need more tomorrow, He'll still be there.

The Fine Print Regarding "Flesh vs. Spirit"

This teaching about "dying to yourself" may sound a little strange if you have not grown up hearing this aspect of the gospel message. Or perhaps you have heard it for many years, but never understood how it applied to you. Do not feel as if you are alone. I was raised in the church, but at twenty-eight years old, this was a new and confusing concept.

I remember preachers from my childhood talking about how life would be wonderful with Christ as my Savior, how heaven was a much better place than hell, and how much God loved me and would bless me if I became one of His followers. It was such a pretty picture, and it sounded so easy—"Come just as you are; ask and ye shall receive; your sins will be washed away, etc., etc.," but they didn't tell me that my sins would wash right back up onto the shore if I didn't die to myself each day! I answered altar calls, one after another, thinking, "Well, the last one must not have done the trick, because I wound up right back in bed with another guy!"

Let me tell you about the fine print to this contract between you and God that doesn't seem to get much fanfare from many churches, because it's not as attractive to newcomers as the "Just ask and ye shall receive" part. I'm referring to the part where, if you desperately desire to live out of righteousness, overcome temptations, and rise to all new spiritual levels in your ability to be a genuine reflection of Christ, you have to kill your flesh (which constantly cries out for earthly pleasures) on a regular basis and yield to the Holy Spirit daily. Allow Him to guide your thoughts, words, and deeds.

If that sounds like a challenge, you are right! Many Christians are forgiven and bound for heaven, but few experience the overcoming life, because few are willing to make the sacrifices required to yield to the Holy Spirit on a day-to-day, moment-by-moment basis. The world has taught us selfishness, not sacrifice! It is time, however, to die to ourselves and let the Potter have His way with the clay. It sounds difficult, but God is in control, and if we will be still, refusing to jump off of the Potter's wheel every time we feel uncomfortable, He will create an incredible masterpiece out of our lives.

As an overcoming Christian, you are merely *in* the world, but no longer *of* the world. In other words, your focus shifts from being like the world to bringing light into the world. This is a challenge that will keep you busy all of your remaining days on earth. Do not be discouraged if you find that you fail to kill your flesh and yield to the Spirit every single time that temptation comes knocking.

Even the Billy Grahams and Mother Teresas of this world struggle to make consistent, conscious decisions to live out of righteousness, but like anything else, it gets easier the more you practice!

Here are some practical examples of "dying to yourself" to put into practice:

1) When you feel tempted to pick up the phone to call him, *don't!* Call *God* instead! *Pray!*

2) When you want to walk out of your way to make sure you cross his path, *don't!* Stay focused on your tasks and find an opportunity to crawl up into God's lap instead!

3) When getting ready in the morning, if you find yourself dressing to impress him, *stop!* Refuse to be a stumbling block to your brother, and dress as if you are going to see God Himself (because you are!).

4) If you find yourself in a face-to-face conversation with him, *think!* Don't say anything that you would not say if Jesus or your current or future spouse were standing right there!

5) If you find yourself thinking about him often throughout the day, *stop!* Memorize Scriptures that you can quote to divert your attention back to God.

6) If you find yourself praying for him too often, *stop!* Pray only for his highest good; do not expound on that prayer, and trust that only God knows what his highest good is and that He will carry that out in His own way and in His own time. Then refuse to allow thoughts of him to monopolize your time with God.

This list of boundaries can grow to meet whatever needs you have. Continue developing it as you are awakened to how your flesh is interfering with your ability to walk in the Spirit. If your life seems to be a living hell of bondage to relationships with men, practicing these principles is crucial to restoring peace and happiness in your life.

Experience Heaven on Earth

Although you are looking forward to heaven someday, why wait for heaven? By living the overcoming life, you can experience heaven on earth as you enjoy these fruits of the Spirit, regain your dignity and wholeness, and witness God's awesome power flowing through you! There is nothing more rewarding than going to bed at night knowing you did your best to live righteously that day, and that you have connected intimately with God and honorably with the people He loves. Can you honestly say you are experiencing heaven on earth? That is exactly what God wants for you, and He will show you how as you continue to kill your flesh and yield to His Spirit.

Jesus tells us, in Luke 9:23, "If anyone would come after Me, he must deny himself and take up his cross daily and follow me." Matthew 10:38–39 also says, "...anyone who does not take his cross and follow Me is not worthy of Me. Whoever finds his life will lose it, and whoever loses his life for My sake will find it." In other words, until you die to yourself, yield to the Spirit, and live an overcoming life, you aren't really "living" at all.

Isn't it time you discovered the life God intended for you to have? Do you want victory over unhealthy relational involvements? Do you want to overcome premarital or extramarital sexual temptations? Do you want to experience the intimacy your heart is truly thirsty for? If your answer to these questions is *yes*, then your neon sign may already be changing from *Woman at the Well* to *Well Woman*!

QUESTIONS FOR INTROSPECTION:

- Have you ever pondered any of the following questions:

    "Why do men go out of their way to talk to me?"
    "Why do men think they can get away with flirting with me?"
    "What is it about me that attracts attention?"
    "Does attracting attention give me a feeling of power or pleasure?"
    "How do I wind up in these compromising situations?"
    "Can men see a neon sign on my forehead? What does it say?"

- What needs to happen in order to allow God to change your neon sign?

- In what ways do you need to "die to your self?"

- What do you think your deepest, innermost needs are?

- How have other men failed to meet these needs in the past?

- Can you trust God to meet your innermost needs in the future? Why, or why not?

- How can you express that trust?

CHAPTER TWO

A Liberating Love

*...that the creation itself will be liberated
from its bondage to decay and brought into the
glorious freedom of the children of God.*
—ROMANS 8:21

So you are ready for some healing water? Let us journey together from Jacob's Well in John, Chapter 4, over to the Pool of Bethesda in John, Chapter 5, where the only question Jesus asks is, "Do you want to get well?" If the answer is yes, then let's jump on in! The water can get a little hot sometimes, but it is healing nonetheless.

> *...Jesus went up to Jerusalem for a feast of the Jews. Now there is in Jerusalem near the Sheep Gate a pool, which in Aramaic is called Bethesda and which is surrounded by five covered colonnades. Here a great number of disabled people used to lie—the blind, the lame, the paralyzed. One who was there had been an invalid for thirty-eight years. When Jesus saw him lying there and learned that he had been in this condition for a long time, He asked him, "Do you want to get well?"*

"Sir," the invalid replied, "I have no one to help me into the pool when the water is stirred. While I am trying to get in, someone else goes down ahead of me."

Then Jesus said to him, "Get up! Pick up your mat and walk." At once the man was cured; he picked up his mat and walked.

The day on which this took place was a Sabbath, and so the Jews said to the man who had been healed, "It is the Sabbath; the law forbids you to carry your mat." But he replied, "The man who made me well said to me, 'Pick up your mat and walk.'"

So they asked him, "Who is this fellow who told you to pick it up and walk?"

The man who was healed had no idea who it was, for Jesus had slipped away into the crowd that was there.

Later Jesus found him at the temple and said to him, "See, you are well again. Stop sinning or something worse may happen to you." The man went away and told the Jews that it was Jesus who had made him well (John 5:1–15).

Notice that the healed man had no revelation of who had actually healed him. When he was questioned, he did not know to whom the credit should be given for such a miracle—he merely knew he could stand on his own two feet again. Later, Jesus found him (indicating that He was "looking" for him in order to make Himself known to this man) and said, "See, you are well again. Stop sinning or something worse may happen to you." This man's inability to give credit where credit was due was a sin. Once Jesus convicted him of that, the man went away and told the Jews that it was Jesus who had made him well. God wanted the glory for this man's healing, and know that He wants the glory for yours as well.

Giving Credit Where Credit is Due

You are probably not quite sure what to expect at this point in the process, but hopefully you were surprised at how much revelation you received from within yourself by answering the "Are You a Woman at the Well?" questionnaire and the questions for introspection in the previous chapter. I want to make sure you understand, early on, W*ho* has begun this healing work in you! Have you given thanks to Jesus Christ for those revelations yet? It is only by *His* stripes that we are healed. Just like the man at the Pool of Bethesda, Jesus wants us to know that He is the one doing the healing and to acknowledge His healing power. You may receive some encouragement from peers, some instruction from counselors or teachers, or some miraculous words of wisdom from a book, but know that these are merely the tools with which God works. Don't give credit to the tool; give credit to the Craftsman! As you continue in this healing process, I encourage you to give all of the glory to God for revelations of truth, for He alone is truth.

The Blame Pit

I am sure you are filled with a plethora of questions at this point. If you are like me, the first question on my mind was, "How did this happen? What happened that drove me to lose my power over temptation and allow my life to get so out of control?" When I asked myself this question, what I really wanted to know was "Who is to blame for this?"

That question itself is a direct reflection of how Satan *wants* us to respond to our own sin. He wants us to blame everyone else and take no personal responsibility for our actions. If he can make you feel "victimized" and hold you in a cell of unforgiveness of your perpetrators, then that is a victory for his side. If you think you are holding someone else prisoner in a cell called "unforgiveness," then there are actually two different cells holding two different prisoners. The other prisoner is you. The key to the cell is being held by the prison guard, Captain Sin.

Remember how you would pray the Lord's Prayer as a child, "And forgive us our trespasses as we forgive others who trespass against us?" That phrase indicates that it is only as we forgive others that we can feel the fullness of Christ's forgiveness of our sins. I've often said, "I know God forgave me, but I find it hard to forgive myself." The underlying truth to that statement was that God had forgiven me, but I personally did not know the fullness of that truth because I had unforgiveness in my own heart toward others. This also caused my self-esteem to remain very low as a result of not knowing the fullness of Christ's forgiveness.

May I encourage you to take the key, unlock the prison cell door, and set your captive free with complete forgiveness? That means they will no longer be in debt to you. You are canceling out their transgression. They owe you nothing. Then and only then will *you* feel justified (which can be translated to mean, "just-if-I'd" never committed those sins!) through your own faith in Christ. Then you can take the key to your prison cell away from Captain Sin and place it in the care of Captain Salvation, becoming a slave of righteousness rather than a slave to your passions!

I share this with you because I don't want you to waste time on a path that ends up in the "blame pit." It is a hard pit to be in, and it leads to nowhere! I wish I could recover the many years I spent closely scrutinizing my father's ability to nurture, digging up every person who had ever done me wrong, and suspecting every man with whom I had ever been involved of being the reason I was so unfulfilled. I thank God that I finally came to the end of that rope, and guess who I found there holding on to it? You guessed it—*me!*

You may think it is easier to blame others for your malady, but this process will go a whole lot more quickly and smoothly if you humble yourself before the Lord and acknowledge that you have played a significant role in your sexual or emotional sin. It takes two to tango, and taking responsibility for your own actions is foundational in your journey toward healing.

Later on you will have the opportunity to examine some of the possible external factors which may have influenced your decisions to succumb to temptations, along with more in-depth exercises on forgiving those who have danced this "tango" along with you, and breaking any soul ties that may remain. But for now, we have to start with you—your previous lack of control over this issue and how it has affected your life.

When Things Start to Spin

Perhaps the term "spinning out of control" means different things to different women. For some, it could mean that you waste countless hours daydreaming about having a love interest in your life. Or perhaps you can't resist calling some special someone, or making sure you run into him as frequently as possible, going out of your way to get his attention. For others, it could mean that it was never your intention to become involved in Internet chat rooms, romance novels (a.k.a. female pornography), or compulsive masturbation, but you find yourself unable to stop these behaviors, attempting to justify them at every turn. Perhaps you realize that you have had more sexual partners than you care to disclose if your friends are bold enough to ask. Or maybe you realized that you were out of control when you heard a medical professional give a talk on sexually transmitted diseases and you wondered, "If there are no symptoms in eighty percent of STD cases, could I be a carrier of one of them and not know it?" Perhaps "out of control" for you means you wound up in the most horrid predicament of your life and had to choose between raising a child as a single parent, coercing a man to marry you, placing your unborn baby up for adoption or choosing to end its life before its birth.

Regardless of how out of control your life has become, how many times do we say, "Just one more time" before we realize there is no such thing? How out of control do our lives have to become before we wake up to the fact that this is not God's will for our lives?

The terror of destroying ourselves any longer brings us to the point of unconditional surrender to God and His will. We have finally come to suspect that the only way to victory in this area of our lives is the only way we haven't already tried—to simply surrender. Finally, we are ready to "Let go and let God" restore order in our chaotic private world.

We Are Not Alone

One of the greatest hindrances to letting God restore order in my own once-chaotic private world was that Satan had me deceived into believing I was the only Christian woman struggling with this issue. In my naive mind, I had the image that Christian women never thought of sex before or outside of marriage. Then there was the opposite extreme—the image judgmentally labeled in my mind as pagan prostitutes who performed sex for money without hesitation or guilt. I knew that I was neither of these extremes, and I was very confused as to where I "fit in." Because it was never discussed or addressed in the church as I was growing up, I had no idea that God created humans to be sexual beings and that as long as we are breathing, we are subject to sexual temptation.

So, because I experienced sexual temptation prior to marriage, I thought there was certainly something very wrong with me. "But I'm a Christian! How can I be struggling with this?" I'd ask myself over and over. However, over the past fourteen years of ministry, God has certainly been faithful to reveal to me that a very small percentage of women can honestly say that they have never been tempted by premarital or extramarital sex (and I wonder if those that would make such a claim are being honest?). At the other extreme, a very small percentage of women actually give away their bodies without hesitation or guilt. The vast majority of us "fit in" somewhere in between, some needing to be more vigilant over their sexual thoughts and behaviors than others because of the possibility of the thought becoming an action, the action becoming a habit, and the habit becoming an addiction.

Facing Ourselves

"Addiction"—*ouch!*—the word itself has such a strong connotation to it. We immediately conjure up images seen in movies, of perverts who molest children or stalk women. As a matter of fact, when we imagine a sex "addict," we most likely imagine a male, not a female, right? But as we take a long, hard, honest look at ourselves, one may begin to wonder... Could a *woman* be addicted to sex and/or relationships? Could a *Christian* woman be addicted to them? Reality begins to sink in.

Again, we want to know how women fall into such a lifestyle. Perhaps definitions of what it means to be addicted to sex and love would help us see how we fall into this abyss, as well as how Jesus Christ can help you climb back out of it. But first, I want to clarify the genre of "addiction." Many professionals have used this term as a diagnosis of what they considered to be a medical condition, but a medical condition is one the patient did not choose and has no control over. I want to adjust your thinking of that word as we journey together down this path toward sexual healing. In our examination of this particular addiction, the word is used to diagnose not a "medical condition," but a "sin condition." Such inward struggles and outward behaviors are a reflection of a sinful condition of the heart. The epitome of the sin we struggle with is failure to be fully dependent on God to satisfy our deepest, innermost needs. In *False Intimacy: Understanding*

the Struggle of Sexual Addiction, Dr. Harry Schaumburg makes the
following statements:

> The essence of sin is autonomy from God, a failure to be depen-
> dent on Him. Sex addicts don't go from being healthy to
> unhealthy because of a disease labeled addiction. Their refusal to
> cling to God as the only Person who can fill their deepest long-
> ings and ease relational pain did not originate in a shame-based
> family but in their shameful, deceitful heart. All of us have such
> a heart.[1]

I often refer to sex and love addiction as a "heart dis-ease." Not
a *disease*, but a *dis-ease*, implying that we are not at ease with the condition of our own heart. And because our heart is experiencing pain,
we have used sex and/or love as a "drug of choice" to ease that pain.

Sex Addiction vs. Love Addiction

The term "addict" is not limited to describing someone who
habitually uses drugs or alcohol, but is defined in *Webster's
Dictionary* as "someone who is devoted to or has surrendered to
something habitually or obsessively." Often "sex addiction" and
"love addiction" are lumped together as one diagnosis ("sex and
love addiction"). However, for our greater understanding, let us
separate the two for a moment.

The term "sex addict" could be defined as one who is devoted
to sex or surrenders to sex habitually or obsessively. The sex addict's
ultimate goal is sex, and he/she will do anything for sex, even if it
means pretending to be in love in order to gain the cooperation of
a sex partner.

The love addict's ultimate goal, however, is love. The term
"love addict" could be defined as one who is devoted to the pursuit
of love or surrenders to relationships habitually or obsessively. The
love addict's ultimate goal is love, and he/she will do anything for

love, even if it requires surrendering sex in order to gain the attention and approval of a potential relational partner. As long as there is a potential for love, there is an even greater potential for vulnerability for the love addict.

With those definitions in mind, you may find yourself leaning more in one direction than another. Because of the way God designed men to be visually stimulated and physically aroused, and women to be emotionally stimulated and relationally aroused (and we'll talk more about God's design of men and women in the next chapter), most men lean toward being sex addicts, while most women lean toward being love addicts. There are certainly exceptions to that philosophy, and there are many men and women who actually are both sex *and* love addicts. But my personal opinion is that if women pursue recovery from "love addiction" (your internal struggle), recovery from "sex addiction" (the outward manifestations of your inward struggle) will take care of itself.

Where do we get this "love" that we are so desperate for? The same place the original Woman at the Well found it... through personal encounters with Jesus Christ. Allowing the Lord to quench your thirst for love with His Living Water will not only change your heart, but will automatically change your behavior.

Love is a Need

If you recognize the fact that you are addicted to love, also recognize that your need for attention, affection, and emotional connection was actually a part of God's plan when He created you. As I was recently talking with a fellow Woman at the Well on a live, call-in radio talk show, she described her plight as, "always having an unhealthy need for love." My response included an explanation that our need for love is anything but unhealthy! God would not place a need for emotional connection in us without a divine purpose and a plan for satisfying that need. The truth of her plight was that she had a healthy need for love (as we all do), but that she had sought to meet that need in some unhealthy ways. You must separate yourself (who God made you to be) from your actions (how you seek to satisfy your needs). You see, Christ longs for you not to be addicted to sex or to love, but to Himself!

Using a similar definition as above, a "Jesus addict" would be described as "someone who is devoted to or has surrendered to Jesus habitually or obsessively." I hope, when others speak of me after I am dead and gone, that they use those exact words. I want to be known as a woman who was totally devoted to Jesus and who surrendered to Him habitually! It is only through that daily devotion and surrender that we discover the sweet satisfaction our hearts long for.

Before we close this chapter of our journey together, I invite you to drink in these deeply profound words from T.D. Jakes' book, *The Lady, Her Lover, and Her Lord*:

> Most men do not associate the giving of their body with the giving of their heart, but women tend to tie the two together. A woman generally offers her body only when she is ready to offer her heart. The giving of her body epitomizes her commitment to her partner. It signifies that she is in love. The virtuous woman values herself too much to be passed around from man to man. Her body generally comes to the altar of love only when there is a safe sense of affection. She will give herself physically only when she is ready to give herself spiritually. Whenever she offers her body, it is an indication that her heart is somewhere close. Yes, her heart lies trembling on the altar; her body is just an announcement that she is serious about her significant other. It signifies her intent to continue the relationship. This is true passion. This is true love. It cannot be demanded or paid for. It comes only when the woman gives it freely and on her own terms. The body and heart combine to form an elixir, the

sweetest wine anyone will ever taste. It is the intoxicating experience that causes a silly grin to emerge on the face of a man in the
middle of the day. It is what makes the woman blush and sigh
softly at her desk. Yes, when a virtuous woman gives her body, she
is also giving her heart and soul. What a treasure to behold!

It is tragic that there are women who have sunk into the
abyss of deplorable lust without love. These women are usually
the victims of an unhealthy upbringing and traumatic experiences that left them wounded with low self-esteem. They don't
value themselves, and thus give their bodies away to anyone who
asks. Or else they use their bodies because they think it is the
only way they can get a man. They think their bodies are the
only things they have to barter with in the game of love. But love
is not a game, nor can it be traded. When a woman gives herself
too easily, she loses worth in the eyes of men. If she doesn't value
herself why should they? But when a woman knows that her
body and her heart are two jewels in the same crown, she will
give that crown only to a man who is worthy. She should give it
only to a prince.[2]

If you do not have a prince of a husband in your life, may I suggest
that you take advantage of this season of singleness in order to
pursue a mad, passionate love affair with the Prince of Peace? Or
even if you have a husband, a love affair with Jesus Christ is an
affair that will only enrich your marriage. The closer two people
come to God, the closer God will bring them together.

Courting Your Creator

The concept of an affair with Jesus may sound totally foreign
to you, but you honestly can have a love relationship with your
Creator that will thrill you, stun you, amaze you, put one of those
silly grins on your face, and make you blush and sigh at your desk!

Do you want to have that kind of affair? Well, start with this concept: All love affairs are carried on in *private*.

As a Christian woman, you probably go to church, but that is a public thing. While corporate worship is important, the kind of intimacy you are pursuing is not the kind you will find surrounded by distractions in a public place. Have you ever courted Him privately, getting down on your knees and worshipping the Maker of the Universe, not because someone instructs you to, but because your heart is so filled with awe? Do you spend time conversing alone with Him, listening for His still, small voice? There is a world of difference between talking *about* God and talking *with* God. Prayer is God's love language! Do you only speak His love language when you need Him to grant you some special favor, or do you commune with Him in fellowship as you would your closest friend? Do you care as much about what He has to say to you as what you have to say to Him? Do you spend time really searching out answers in Scripture? Have you memorized any verses that remind you of the kind of love only He has for you?

Forget looking for a knight in shining armor! You have a Savior who withstood torture to the point of death on a cross just so He could make a special place for *you* at His side in heaven for all eternity. Forget trying to find a man to support you financially. The Lord has a mansion built for you in glory and He has paved your street with gold.

Have you, like many other women, spent years with only a Sunday-school knowledge of God while earning an honorary doctorate in self-indulgence, self-pity, and self-destruction? Sweet Princess, it is time to die to yourself and enter into the throne room of love and grace, where the Everlasting Prince eagerly awaits your time, your attentions and your affections.

Listen, O daughter, consider and give ear: Forget your people and your father's house. The King is enthralled by your beauty; honor Him, for He is your lord. All glorious is the princess within her chamber; her gown is interwoven with gold. In embroidered garments she is led to the King; her virgin companions follow her and are brought to You. They are led in with joy and gladness; they enter the palace of the King (Psalm 45:10–11, 13–15).

QUESTIONS FOR INTROSPECTION:

• What are the signs that your sexual or emotional life may be out of control?

• What effect does your "out of control" life have on you? On others?

• Have you fallen into the "blame pit"? Is there someone you are holding in a prison cell of unforgiveness?

• Do you believe that God is the only one who can satisfy your deepest longings?

• In what ways are you pursuing a private love affair with the Lord?

• What things do you want to incorporate in your daily life to enhance this heavenly affair?

CHAPTER THREE

Back to the Blueprints

And God saw all that He had made
and it was very good.
—GENESIS 1:31

A Korean student at Liberty University recently asked me in broken English this very insightful question: "Why in your country is sex so, so, so... *okay* to talk about everywhere... in American movies and magazines... but *not okay* to talk about in American church?"

I've been asking that question for years! How can we understand this complex gift of sexuality we have been given unless we look to the Author of sex to discover what He had in mind? It is time to consult the Creator, go back to the blueprints, and reconstruct! There we can remove all of our misconceptions—about ourselves, about men, about sex, and about love—in order to allow God to build into us all that He wants us to know and understand about His creation.

Surely, had we seen ourselves and others through God's eyes in the first place, we would not have abused our sexuality or allowed it to be abused as a result of our own ignorance. We would have cherished our bodies as temples of the Holy Spirit. We would never have cheapened and squandered this most precious gift God gave to us.

Squandering Our Sexuality

While visiting my parents recently, I was introduced to a television program where people brought old treasures that they had found and could inquire of an antique dealer as to their exact worth. One woman brought a beautiful ruby brooch that her mother had purchased in 1955 for her to play dress-up with as a child. Her mother had paid fifty cents for the brooch. The antique dealer examined it and determined that it was, in fact, a *real* ruby and that "Cartier" was inscribed on the back of the tarnished gold setting in barely distinguishable letters. The owner was ecstatic to discover that her brooch was valued at over $10,000! My first thought was, "What a shame the original owner had no idea what a treasure the brooch actually was! Imagine giving that treasure away for only fifty cents!"

But isn't that what many of us do with our treasure, our virginity—the most precious and holy gift God could give us? So many of us have just given it away to the first customer willing to pay some attention for it. Oh, if we had just realized the incredible value of it!

Refusing to beat ourselves up over our past misconceptions, however, we can allow these experiences to be our teachers of the greatest lessons in life. When we recognize that it is, in fact, this sin, repentance from this sin, and a desperate desire to avoid this sin in the future that causes us to seek God in a way we never have before, we then can become grateful for these experiences. We may have suffered over the misuse of our sexuality, but that suffering often puts us on a pathway toward God.

Realize that being a sinner in desperate pursuit of holiness, righteousness, and a real relationship with the one true God is, in fact, a very good thing. God loves brokenness, because His power is made perfect only in our weakness. If we thought we were plenty strong enough to fight this battle for sexual purity and sanity on our own, we wouldn't think we needed God. But recognizing our failures to gain victory in this area of our lives opens the door for Christ's final victory to be ours. Our sin died on that cross when Christ did. And His victory over death and Satan was our victory over spiritual death and Satan's temptations.

Many of our mistakes were born out of our misconceptions or the faulty way we view things. Matthew 6:22–23 says,

> *The eye is the lamp of the body. If your eyes are good, your whole body will be full of light. But if your eyes are bad, your whole body will be full of darkness. If then the light within you is darkness, how great is that darkness!*

I want to make sure our eyes are seeing things in a Godly light, so that our whole body will be full of light. Let us expose some of Satan's lies that have kept us blinded to God's truths about sexuality.

No Guy-Bashing Allowed!

The first of Satan's lies I want to expose is that all men are "pigs" and that they are all after one thing—sex. As the daughter, sister, wife, mother, coworker, and friend of many respectable Christian men, I take personal offense when I hear women talk that way about God's creation. Sadly, there *are* some men who look to ease their own pain by pursuing sexual relations with any willing (and unfortunately, sometimes unwilling) partners. But sisters, let's not deceive ourselves by thinking for one minute that Christ had to hang longer on the cross for their sin than for our own.

I was listening to a Christian talk show one afternoon and the topic was, "What is your response to *Sports Illustrated's* annual swimsuit edition?" Almost every male caller claimed to believe the magazine was pornography and had thrown it in the trash where it belonged. Many called in to say they had cancelled their subscriptions to *Sports Illustrated* because they felt such rage toward the publication's degradation of women.

Listening to these responses affirmed my belief that the majority of Christian men do not want to be tempted, respect women, and earnestly try to keep their sexual thoughts and behaviors in check. But so often a woman longing to conquer a challenging counterpart, in order to affirm the power of her sexual prowess, makes it extremely difficult for these men to be successful in their vigilance. And then when we succeed at our sexual or emotional conquest, we too often place the blame spotlight on *his* lack of control! It seems as if we've been brainwashed into thinking that *men* are the cause of our struggles with our *own* sexual behavior!

But in order to allow light to drive out such darkness, let's back up to the creation story in the first chapter of Genesis (which must be a very important message for God to have included it in the first chapter in the first Book of the Bible!). There we will examine what God had in mind when He designed two such similar, yet completely different creatures.

Progenitors vs. Nurturers

Imagine Adam and Eve in the garden. God gives them the command, "Be fruitful and increase in number." Basically, that was a two-part command: have sex and make babies.

Now, if all Adam wanted to do was walk in the garden holding hands with Eve and sharing his innermost thoughts and feelings, would they have ever gotten around to having sex? Probably not. God placed in Adam an ability to be sexually aroused simply at the sight of Eve's beauty, in order that he would *want* to obey God's command to "multiply and increase in number." It is not that men are pigs with only one thing on their mind, but that God gave men the incredible responsibility of being the *progenitor* of the human race. God placed in man exactly what he would need in order to fulfill that responsibility—the desire to be physically intimate.

Now, if all Eve wanted to do was chase Adam and have sex, work in the fields, arm wrestle, and play football, would she have raised healthy, well-balanced, sensitive children? Probably not. But God placed in Eve the desire to be emotionally connected and the desire to be involved in emotionally caring for and nurturing others. God wanted Eve to obey His command to "be fruitful" and to sow seeds to help others grow. It is not that women are frigid or just like to tease guys. It is that God gave them the incredible responsibility of being the *nurturers* of the human race. He placed in them exactly what they would need to fulfill that responsibility—the desire to be emotionally intimate.

God also gave Adam and Eve the ability to communicate, share experiences, and relate to one another. God created them for one another's pleasure, and that pleasure is sometimes emotional, sometimes physical, sometimes mental, and sometimes spiritual. Therefore, in a marriage relationship when the two become one flesh, that "one-flesh union" creates an emotional, physical, mental, and spiritual bond. Ideally, the husband strives to be more emotionally connected, although it may not be his primary nature. The wife strives to make herself more physically available to her husband because she understands that God has created him with such a need, and she wants to be the source of his physical fulfillment. As the years go by, their connections grow stronger as they strive to recognize and meet one another's needs and protect their marriage relationship from outside emotional or physical temptations.

Therefore, in God's economy, men are responsible for ensuring the continuation of the human race. Women are responsible for nurturing this human race. And God gave each of us the exact emotional and physical makeup we would need in order to fulfill this commission. He designed men and women with a distinct plan in mind, and it is certainly a divine one that has been successful through hundreds of generations!

Love Does Not Equal Sex

I find it ironic that women who settle for premarital sex are usually not even looking for sex. They are looking for love. But this fallen world we live in has convinced so many that love equals sex. Frequently I hear women say to me, "I thought that if I had sex with him, then he would love me and stay with me." There are many Women at the Well whose testimony includes the thought that if a man wanted to have sex with her, it must have meant that she was irresistible and he was madly in love with her. Those same women have attended the weddings of many sex partners, but never as the bride.

The truth is that love does not equal sex, and sex will not satisfy a woman's need for love. No lust is ever satisfying, whether it is for money, fame, power, or sex. That is why I call it "stagnant water." One taste only leaves you thirsty for another, then another, but regardless of how much stagnant water you drink, you will still be thirsty. Only the love of God is fully satisfying. Only Living Water quenches the thirst of your soul.

So, if love does not equal sex, how do you recognize the difference between them? The difference is *commitment*. Any man can give you sex without commitment, but it is a pearl of great price that will give you a commitment without sex. If a man is willing to sacrifice his own pleasure before marriage, cherish sexual purity, and protect your own dignity and reputation, then he is a man who truly loves you.

Also keep in mind that if he is strong enough to resist the urge to have sex with the woman he wants to spend the rest of his life with, you can bet he is strong enough to resist the urge to ever defile your marriage bed with another woman. Because to him, love equals commitment. He is only able to love the one to whom he is truly committed.

To Be or Not To Be a Sex Object?

Still another one of Satan's lies is that women are sex objects. You may be thinking, "Of course they are not! I know that already!" but do you really? To what extent do you attempt to imitate the so-called "sexy" women that you see on television? How hard do you try to have the figure of a fashion model? How much money do you spend each month on cosmetics, hairstyling, fitness club memberships, clothing, etc., to make your body, face, hair, nails, etc., more attractive to a man?

I'm certainly not saying that it is wrong to be or want to be attractive. Again, our bodies are holy temples and we should keep them clean, healthy, and attractive. But how much of your time and income is dedicated to having "the look" that Satan has deceived you into thinking you need? Is it really your desire to look like a beauty queen, or have you fallen into the trap of believing that the only way to attract a man is by luring him in with "the look?"

Matthew 6:21 says, "For where your treasure is, there your heart will be also." I'd like to rephrase that by saying, "For wherever your treasure goes, that is an indication of where your heart already is!" Do you spend more money on glamour than on glory? Do you lay more money down at the cosmetics counter than you do in the offering plate? Have you provided a better living for your personal trainer than for the missionaries in your church? Do you invest in physical beauty that is fleeting rather than spiritual beauty, which is everlasting?

Proverbs 31:30 says, "Charm is deceptive, and beauty is fleeting; but a woman who fears the Lord is to be praised." Once you let go of the idea in your head that you must have "the look" to catch a man, you can have more time to focus on the things that really matter: gaining dignity and self-respect out of the knowledge that you are a co-worker with God himself! God can use you to impact many lives for eternity, but not if you have your eyes focused solely on yourself and the possibility of a man at your side. Ask Jesus to be the one to come alongside you, and He will guide you into viewing yourself not as a glamour girl or a sex object, but as a daughter of royalty. As a child of the King, focus not on how beautiful you look in your royal robe, but on advancing your Father's Kingdom.

The Lost Art of Modesty

One of the most important virtues a woman can strive to possess is a sense of modesty. It seems to have been lost in our society over the past several decades. You certainly don't see modesty portrayed much on television, in the movies, or on the cover of magazines! Just about every form of media you can think of has shredded the importance of modesty in women's minds, and as a result, shredded the importance of sexual propriety. What is the devastating effect on our society of such a loss of modesty and propriety? Sisters, we are causing our brothers to stumble and fall into sexual temptation. Luke 17:1–3 says:

> *Things that cause people to sin are bound to come, but woe to that person through whom they come. It would be better for* [her] *to be thrown into the sea with a millstone tied around* [her] *neck than for* [her] *to cause* [a man] *to sin.*

Isn't that a sobering thought? When I first heard that passage of Scripture, I began to understand that God really wanted me to get a strong hold on this concept of modesty.

Many envision a modest woman as being overweight, unattractive, or embarrassed because of her looks, but modesty is anything but being uncomfortable with one's looks. It is defined as

(1) freedom from conceit or vanity or (2) propriety in dress, speech, or conduct. If anything, modesty is being comfortable enough with your looks that you do not feel the need to flaunt them! As my husband told me early in our marriage, as I was trying on different styles of skirts, "Shannon, the longer skirts are much more becoming. I know you have nice legs, but everyone else doesn't need to know that!"

When a woman dresses appropriately, speaks appropriately, and conducts herself appropriately, not only is she respected by others, but she is honored by God. Katie Luce, co-founder of Teen Mania Ministries and wife of author and speaker Ron Luce, teaches women that if you view your self with respect and honor, it will carry over into every area of your life. She gives a powerful example of walking into a female locker room. You can walk through that restricted area and probably recognize which women are careful to honor God with their bodies and which are much more vulnerable to sexual immorality. The key to such discernment is to watch for modesty. Women who do not flaunt their bodies in public usually treat them as a holy temple in private as well. Katie encourages women to focus their efforts on establishing a strong sense of modesty by examining (1) their attitude, (2) their dress, and (3) their words.

Sporting an Attitude

Isn't it funny how you can determine peoples' attitudes merely by watching their mannerisms? You can actually *see* their attitude displaying itself in the way they walk, the way they talk, the way that they look at you (in the eye, or up and down your body, or over your shoulder). Try this test: next time you are standing in line in a fast-food restaurant, watch the service person behind the counter. Notice mannerisms. Does she or he look customers in the eye? Does the server keep glancing behind customers at someone else in line, or does he or she look down at the register the whole time? Does this person hold his or her head up to speak, and speak loudly or softly? Is the order filled efficiently and confidently, or does the server drag her or his heels behind the counter? Does he or she run around like a chicken with its head cut off, while screaming at the cook for not being fast enough? You can determine a person's attitude just by watching for a few moments—whether they enjoy their job, whether they take pride in serving you with courtesy, whether they are confident in their ability to perform, etc.

Our attitudes are just as visible to others. And when women carry themselves with the attitude, "Ain't I something to look at!" many undesirable men will certainly look in that direction. Most respectable men recognize that a woman with an immodest attitude is really one whose self-esteem has rotted away. She feels such a lack of confidence that she searches outside herself for the affirmation she cannot find within. She feels so helplessly out of control that she uses her seductive power to try to gain control over a man.

You may not think others can recognize what is really going on inside of you, but it is written all over your attitude. Your countenance—or the way you carry yourself—teaches people how to treat you. If you don't respect yourself, why should anyone else? If, however, your attitude is one of respect for yourself and for others (including your Christian brothers who are trying to avoid temptation), then others will show you the same respect.

Dressed to Impress

The fashion industry has done more to warp women's sense of modesty than any other factor, in my opinion. Regardless of the season, the style as of late is usually short, tight, or as revealing as possible. Clothes are leaving less and less to the imagination and luring more and more women into sexual promiscuity.

Sure, it is easy to say that it's the guy's fault for chasing you, but sweetheart, please ask yourself, "What kind of bait do I use?" You see, you don't catch a trout using catfish bait, and you don't catch a godly man using Satan's bait. If you dress seductively in order to catch a man, you are going to catch a lustful one. And keep in mind that the way that you attract him is also the way you are going to have to keep him. If you dress like his little plaything, that is exactly what you will be. And another little plaything may come across his path down the road to give you a run for your money.

If you want to catch a respectable, faithful, godly man, then *you* have got to show yourself as a respectable, faithful, godly woman. Make a comprehensive list of the characteristics you would like in a husband. Once your list is complete, go back down the list and ask yourself, "Which of those characteristics do *I* already possess?" You are going to catch what you advertise for, and if godliness is one of the characteristics you desire in a husband, make sure you are advertising godliness. Invite a friend over to help you go through your closet and get rid of clothes that serve as Satan's bait. From now on, clothe your body not with the latest fashion, but with the greatest fashion—*modesty!*

The Power of a Word

Again, turning back to the creation story in the first chapter of Genesis, all of the wonders that God created were formed by His mere words. John 1:1 states, "In the beginning was the Word and the *Word* was with God and the *Word* was God," implying that the *Word* itself was the ultimate original source and had the power to form creation.

As a desensitized generation, we often fail to recognize the power of words. With a simple word, we can be wind underneath people's wings, causing them to soar to their greatest heights. We can also rip someone to shreds with our words, scarring them for life. As Women at the Well, we need to be vigilant of every word that comes out of our mouths, especially in the presence of men.

Ephesians 4:29 says, "Let no corrupt communication proceed out of your mouth, but that which is good to the use of edifying, that it may minister grace unto the hearers."

We also have great power to tempt others with our words. Would you like to know what a four letter word for "foreplay" is? T-A-L-K! Ask any predator what their secret for luring in their prey is. Their secret is in their conversation. Every affair begins with intimate words. If you are careful to avoid private conversations, inappropriate words to fall on your ears, or suggestive language to come out of your mouth, then you are exercising your power to stop an affair long before it happens! A good rule of thumb is to speak only words that you would speak if Jesus were standing next to you... because He really is!

A New Creation

"Therefore, if anyone is in Christ, [she] is a new creation; the old has gone, the new has come!" (2 Corinthians 5:17.) Believing that God is taking us back to His blueprints and reconstructing us as new creations, it is time to come out of the cocoon of your misconceptions about your self, men, sex and love!

Just imagine what a testimony you will be to others when they recognize the new way in which you carry yourself. You have a fuller understanding of how God created men and women, and you respect yourself and others. You treat your body as a holy temple, dressing it modestly. No unwholesome talk comes out of your mouth. You are no longer focused on getting the love you once craved, but on giving the love of Christ that others are craving.

You are a new creation, so spread your beautiful wings and soar to new heights!

QUESTIONS FOR INTROSPECTION:

• What are some of the misconceptions you have held about yourself?

About men?

About sex?

About love?

• What are some of the revelations God has given you about yourself?

About men?

About sex?

About love?

• Do you carry yourself in a way that demands respect? How so?

• Do you demonstrate respect to others? How so?

• In what ways have you been a stumbling block to men in the past?

• How can you avoid repeating that same pattern?

• To what new heights could you soar if you went back to God's blueprints and reconstructed your life accordingly?

CHAPTER FOUR

The Sin that Dwells Within

I do not understand my own actions. For I do not do what I want,
but I do the very thing I hate... I can will what is right,
but I cannot do it. For I do not do the good I want,
but the evil I do not want is what I do. Now if I do what I do not
want, it is no longer I that do it, but sin which dwells within me.
—ROMANS 7:15–20

One day a friend was driving down the road with her three children in the back seat of the car. She was reprimanding her son for giving in to the temptation of picking on his younger sisters. After contemplating his mother's correction for a few moments (and possibly reflecting on a sermon or two he had heard his dad preach from the pulpit), the young boy responded profoundly, "I sure wish Adam and Eve had not bitten that apple!"

Isn't that the truth? Wouldn't it be great if we could go back to the way things were in the Garden of Eden, and live in complete bliss and in perfect union with God and with each other? Since we were young children, most of us have heard the story about how Paradise was lost when Eve gave in to the serpent's temptation to take a bite of the forbidden fruit. But I wonder if there weren't some things brewing in Eve's heart even before she took the first bite.

Let's look at some of the details behind the Fall of Man (Genesis 3). Imagine the cunning serpent hissing in Eve's ear, "Did God really say, 'You must not eat from *any* tree in the garden'?" (Genesis 3:1) He added to what God actually said in Genesis 2:16–17 (that she must not eat from the tree of knowledge of good and evil). In her response, Eve seems to fall for the serpent's trick. She, too, adds to what God actually said by replying, "We may eat fruit from the trees in the garden, but God did say, 'You must not eat fruit from the tree that is in the middle of the garden, *and you must not touch it*, or you will die.'" (Genesis 3:2–3) God never said that she must not touch it. He said that she must not eat of it. The serpent proceeds with his deceptive ploy and tells her, "You will not surely die, for God knows that when you eat of it your eyes will be opened and you will be like God, knowing good and evil" (Genesis 4).

Confused by Satan's scheme, Eve fell into the same trap that many of us fall into today. She took her eyes off of the Creator and focused, instead, on the creation. "Ooh," she must have thought. "I could have the same wisdom as God?" And in her desire to be like God, or even a "god" herself, she pursued God's gifts of wisdom and knowledge rather than pursuing God Himself. Isn't that, in essence, selfishness? Arrogance? Pride? Correct on all charges. Although she had been given perfect surroundings by the perfect Provider, Eve selfishly wanted a promotion. She arrogantly assumed that she was entitled to something that she had not been given yet. Feeling as if she deserved to be like God, pride came before her fall. The internal sinful condition of Eve's heart led her to succumb to the external temptation of taking that bite.

Not wanting to be alone in her sin, it was also Eve's selfishness that led her to give her husband a bite as well. Perhaps she thought that two wrongs would make a right, but such is never the case. Adam and Eve once frolicked in the garden unashamed and unaware of anything more blissful (because there wasn't). But because they did not trust God's goodness (as if He had been holding something back from them) they greedily sought more by their own means. As a result, things no longer appeared perfect. Their eyes were opened to their nakedness and they hid in shame. Have you ever felt that you could not enter into His presence because of your guilt? Have you been playing hide-and-seek with God?

Mercifully, God sought Adam and Eve, fully aware of what they had done. He offered them a chance to confess, and clothed their nakedness with fig leaves. God also searches for us, fully aware of our sin. He longs to hear our confessions, and desires to clothe us once again with dignity and restoration. God doesn't want us to hide. He seeks to be in fellowship once again with us. He misses us like crazy when we go astray.

If Eve had examined the sin dwelling within her heart just before taking that catastrophic bite, what would she have discovered? If she had recognized the error of her thinking, would it have helped her look to God to satisfy her desire for wisdom rather than falling prey to the serpent's schemes? While we will never know for sure, I know that recognizing the things that are operating in my own heart and reconciling those issues early (prior to acting out in sin) have been a great deterrent of the enemy. The best defense against the devil is to know his tactics. They have not changed at all. He still hisses into the ears of women, attempting to lure them away from the Creator (God) and focus on the creation instead (men). Satan hates women and is in the world seeking to steal our hearts, kill our consciences, and destroy our self-esteem. But my friends, greater is He that is in us (Christ) than he that is in the world (Satan) (1 John 4:4).

While you may be fearful of what you will see if you ask God to turn on His searchlight for any sin that dwells within your heart, continue to remind yourself that this is one of the most positive steps toward actual change. And isn't change our goal? If we know that we are not yet what God desires us to be, or what we want to be ourselves, how can we avoid investigating those things requiring change in order for us to be transformed into His image? As 2 Corinthians 3:18 says, "We are being transformed into His likeness with ever increasing glory." As we invite God to search our hearts and reveal our innermost sinful thoughts that lead us into temptation, we will be transformed into a greater likeness of Christ and our lives will bring more glory to God.

Internal Factors that Drive

In his writings about what causes sexual addiction, Dr. Harry Schaumburg masterfully cuts to the heart issues governing the behavior of sex and love addicts in *False Intimacy: Understanding the Struggle of Sexual Addiction*—

> Unless treatment programs address people's deceitfulness and rebellion of the heart, they can't deal with the fundamental issue underlying sexually addictive behaviors. To take any other position is to say, in essence, "Sin can be dealt with apart from what Christ did for us on the cross."[1]

Schaumburg's discussion of internal factors which drive external behaviors include arrogance and pride, selfishness, and fear of pain.

Pride Comes Before a Fall

Women at the Well have a tendency to look to earthly outlets to plug into, attempting to satisfy what they perceive as their own needs. They feel the need for belonging and for connection, so they look for a man to belong to or a partner to connect with. Rather than finding satisfaction in their role as a beloved daughter who belongs to a Heavenly Father or a virtuous bride who lives in connection with her Sacred Groom, the Woman at the Well seeks to create her own connection, her own place of belonging. Although she may never openly admit it, she assumes that waiting on God to satisfy her innermost needs would either take too long or end fruitlessly, so she plays by her own rules and devises her own schemes.

She thinks she knows what she needs, and therefore creates a list of "things she wants in a man," all the while ignorant of the fact that what she really needs is what no man can provide. She drinks stagnant water, relationship after relationship, seeking a taste of heaven by her own means, but creating a living hell of uncontrolled desires instead. She is like a greedy pirate digging for treasure, completely independent of any reliable treasure map. Oh, how God longs to show her His map! How He desires to show you the treasure He holds in the very palm of His hand!

Selfishness

Women at the Well also have a history of insisting that their needs be met on demand, regardless of who it affects. She walks into a room and wants heads to turn. She desires to be the center of attention. She can't have a good time in a social setting unless she is the most attractive woman there. She has to have a story to tell. She lives to enlighten everyone about herself and what is going on in her life, but has little interest in what is going on in the lives of others. She seeks to satisfy her burning passions, even if her flame burns someone else.

In his convicting book, *I Was Always On My Mind*, Steve Sampson claims that a good gauge to measure self-centeredness is to examine your prayer life. He asks, "How much do you pray? What percentage of your prayers are directed toward the needs of others and for the increase of the Kingdom of God?"[2]. If you find that your prayers are mostly centered around *you*, Sampson suggests that you repent, for such hinders the flow of the Holy Spirit to work in other's lives. James 5:16 says, "Pray for one another, that you may be healed," leading us to believe that our own healing comes from taking our eyes off our ourselves and looking to the needs of others. When you are focused on other people's needs, your own needs don't seem so extreme after all.

Fear of Pain

If you were hesitant to read this particular chapter, or even pick up this book, for that matter, ask yourself why—why did you hesitate? What did you fear?

It is often said that the truth hurts. Many women attempt to avoid such pain at all costs, thinking that if they don't face the truth, then it can't actually be truth. But truth is absolute, whether we face it or not, and it is time for Women at the Well to face whatever pain they have been attempting to mask through their use of fantasy and their incessant search for ecstasy.

Where "escape" has been goal number one for too long, recognizing our sin is our new goal. You may not have considered "fear" a sin before, but fear is the opposite of faith, and if we fear our reality, then we do not have faith that God will help us cope with our reality. We do not trust that God can truly meet our innermost needs. Affirmation and acceptance are among the innermost needs of all women, but rather than recognizing God's affirmation and acceptance of us, or waiting on God's timing to bring affirmation and acceptance to us through a healthy relationship, we impatiently create fantasies in order to imagine the affirmation and acceptance that we crave. Upon the discovery of how pleasurable this affirmation and acceptance is (even though it is only fantasized at this point), we become so enamored with its ability to provide escape and ecstasy that we begin to fear that we will never actually experience it in a real relationship.

Those fantasies, coupled with the fear of never finding ultimate fulfillment, lead us to depend on our own strategies for self-fulfillment and, as a result, masturbation often becomes the way we avoid our fear of pain and arrogantly provide our own ecstasy. Some

Christians have argued, "But masturbation is not specifically mentioned in the Bible. Because it involves no one else, it can't be wrong." However, I challenge that assumption. Most women report that orgasm (or the most intense state of sexual arousal) is approximately five percent physical and ninety-five percent mental for them. In other words, physical stimulation is certainly a necessary ingredient to orgasm, but if a woman's mind is somewhere else (on her shopping list, for example), orgasm will never occur as a result of just the physical stimulation by itself. It requires focused mental involvement. For married women, this means focusing on your husband and your passionate love relationship with him. But for an unmarried woman, such mental focus would require intimate thoughts of a man who is not your husband. These types of thoughts are referred to as "lust" in Scripture. Matthew 5:27–28 says, "You have heard that it was said, 'Do not commit adultery.' But I tell you that anyone who looks at [or thinks about] a woman [or a man] lustfully has already committed adultery with her [or him] in their own heart." If you doubt this theory at all, ask yourself honestly, "Have I ever masturbated without thinking lustful thoughts of someone I was not already married to?" The two go hand in hand, and therefore both should be avoided.

But if we continue such a pattern of self-gratification, we endanger ourselves of becoming so prideful and independent about the fulfillment of our own sexual needs that it becomes too difficult to trust anyone else to meet those same needs. When our husbands are given the opportunity to be the source of our sexual pleasure, we have already undermined their efforts. For example, a woman may become frustrated with her husband during sex and think, "He doesn't know what he is doing. He doesn't have a clue how to please me." Most men are willing to learn how to please their wives, but if you have repeatedly used masturbation as a means of self-gratification, you are right. He has no clue how you have pleasured yourself or how other men have pleasured you in the past. When you compare your husband's sexual abilities to your own abilities to please yourself or to a previous partner's abilities, you are dooming your husband to fail at ever sexually satisfying you. Had you never "practiced" sexual pleasure outside of marriage, the two of you could have found incredible fulfillment exploring this pleasure together—learning, teaching, and bonding together in a one-flesh union.

As a result of such sexual frustration, the intimacy we have longed for via fantasy may never become a reality, because we often perpetuate this vicious cycle by:

1) failing to realize that only God can fulfill us completely,

2) fearing that we will never be fulfilled by another,

3) finding "imaginary fulfillment" through fantasy,

4) translating "imaginary fulfillment" into some form of "actual fulfillment" through the use of masturbation or pre-marital sex,

5) becoming sexually self-sufficient to the point of independence from our husbands and from God.

If this vicious cycle sounds to you as if it leads to isolation and resentment rather than intimacy and fulfillment, you are exactly right. However, with God's help we can face our fears rather than seeking to escape from them through the use of fantasy and masturbation. These fears, isolation, and resentment can be overcome because we serve a God who can overcome anything. If He can overcome death and the grave, He can help us overcome these things as well.

Other Defects that Drive

In addition to pride, selfishness, and fear, there are many other examples of internal factors that I feel are crucial to mention.

Rather than describe them, it might be more effective if you were to hear examples of them. The following questions are based on emotions or character flaws that many Women at the Well claim were behind much of their sexual exploits. In asking yourself these questions, perhaps you can get a better idea of some of the internal factors that may have driven you in the past:

PRIDE / ARROGANCE:

Have you pursued someone in order to see if you could conquer their resolve to remain sexually pure? Have you had sex regardless of the consequences, feeling as if consequences will "never happen" to you?

POWER / CONTROL:

Have you ever attempted to see how many different partners you could involve in your sexual exploits or to see how many times you could involve one particular sexual partner? Have you ever tried to "drive someone crazy" with kissing or foreplay, with no intention of going all the way? Do you feel bored or uneasy unless there is someone around with whom you can flirt?

SELFISHNESS:

Have you ever pursued sex because you felt that you were entitled to pleasure? Have you ever threatened your reputation or someone else's in order to pursue a relationship or sex? Do you feel that your sexual and/or romantic life affects your spiritual life in a negative way?

FEAR:

Have you had sex because you were afraid that your partner would leave you if you didn't? Have you found yourself in a relationship that you cannot leave? Have you used sex and/or relationships to try to deal with or escape from life's problems?

REJECTION / REVENGE:

Have you ever had sex in order to medicate the pain of someone else rejecting you? Have you ever had sex with one man in order to get even with another one? Have you used a sexual relationship with one man in order to get even with your father for not providing the attention you craved as a child? Do you attempt to compete with your mother, sister or friends to prove you can get a better boyfriend?

LOW SELF-ESTEEM / INSECURITY:

Have you ever had sex in order to feel accepted or attractive? Do you think that sex or a relationship will make your life bearable? Are most of your closest friends males rather than females? Do you feel desperate about your need for a boyfriend or a future husband? Do you find you have a pattern of repeating bad relationships? Do you feel that your major value in a relationship is your ability to perform sexually? Do you feel that life would have no meaning without a love relationship or without sex? Do you need to have sex or "fall in love" in order to feel like a "real woman"? Do you find the pain and desperation in your life increasing no matter what you do? Do you feel as if you could never be truly acceptable to others? Do you feel that you lack dignity and wholeness?

GREED / AMBITION:

Have you ever had sex with someone who had power (i.e., a boss, a teacher, or someone in authority) in order to gain favor or power for yourself? Have you ever had sex for money? Have you ever pursued a relationship in hopes of gaining status or a promotion?

PITY:

Have you ever had sex with someone because you felt sorry for him? Have you ever pursued a relationship with someone because you thought he was a "diamond in the rough?" Do you seek out men who need to be "fixed" or who you think need your love?

REBELLION:

Have you ever wanted to "take a walk on the wild side?" Have you ever gone to a club or a social scene that you normally would not involve yourself in? Have you ever wanted to have sex or pursue a relationship with someone that everyone else warns you to stay away from?

IGNORANCE:

Have you ever pursued a relationship with someone without knowing why? Have you ever had sex with someone because you did not know how else to end the date or get him to leave? Have you found yourself in compromising situations without knowing how you got there?

HABIT:

Do you find yourself flirting with someone even if you do not mean to? Is sex a routine part of your romantic relationships? Do you have sex habitually because it is just "something that you do?" Do you keep a list in your head of the number of partners you have had? Have you found yourself unable to stop seeing a guy even if you know that seeing him is destructive to you? Do you feel the urge to have sex whenever you are feeling hungry, angry, lonely, tired, or bored?

Who Does Sin Hurt?

As Christians, we often use God's mercy as a crutch, depending on it so heavily that we are not inspired to change. In other words, many of us have the idea that "It is okay for me to commit this sin again because God will forgive me." While it is certainly true that

God does love us and forgives us repeatedly for our sins, let's not take His mercy for granted by treating it as a license to remain entrenched in sin. God is quick to forgive, but don't fool yourself into thinking that it is "okay with Him" if we sin. Sin rips God's heart out. He can't stand to see His children stumble and fall, and He grieves and weeps for His wayward daughters. But God lets us make our own choices, because He loved us enough to give us free will—the freedom to choose whether we follow Him or our own selfish desires. Imagine that—God loves us so much that He would rather see us have the freedom to turn away from Him than to force us to turn toward Him. Just like any other suitor, God wants us to *want* to please Him. He wants us to *want* to obey Him. He wants us to avoid sin at all costs, because we know what it does to Him (and to us). Sin was such a major issue with God that He chose to sacrifice His one and only Son in order for us to have victory over it. And sin is still a major issue for God. Therefore, it is a major issue for you.

You see, not only do you hurt God when you sin, you hurt yourself.

> *Flee from sexual immorality. All other sins a man commits are outside his body, but he who sins sexually sins against his own body. Do you not know that your body is a temple of the Holy Spirit, who is in you, whom you have received from God? You are not your own; you were bought at a price. Therefore honor God with your body* (1 Corinthians 6:18).

When we fail to honor God with our bodies, we suffer many consequences. Physically, we subject ourselves to pregnancy and disease. Mentally, we subject ourselves to the anguish of replaying in our minds over and over the magnitude of our sin. Emotionally, we suffer the pain of yet another failed relationship and damaged self-esteem. But spiritually is where we suffer the most harm. You see, God cannot be in the presence of sin. Sure, we all have sins of omission (failing to do something that we should) and sins of commission (doing something that we should not) that have not been brought to our conscience yet. When the Holy Spirit reveals that we have unconfessed sin in our lives and yet we fail to be repentant, we push God further and further away. Fortunately for us, God can never be pushed so far away that we can't turn from our ways and run right back into His loving arms again in order to experience the fullness of complete fellowship with Him.

If you are not enjoying the fullness of complete fellowship with your Creator, begin searching your heart to discover any unconscious sin and then seek to understand how it may serve as an internal drive toward your external behaviors. Once these drives are recognized and understood, their power over you is as good as gone. We can't overcome darkness with our eyes closed, but we can overcome darkness when we open the eyes of our hearts and allow God to shed His light on what's really operating within us. By setting out on such a quest to discover the sin that dwells within, we stand in agreement with God about our need for His mercy and grace, and we free the Holy Spirit to begin His good work in us.

 QUESTIONS FOR INTROSPECTION:

• What internal factors do you recognize operating in your own heart that drive you toward unacceptable behaviors?

- Have you ever felt as if you know what you need, in your life or in a relationship, better than God knows?

- Do you use masturbation as a way of escaping relational pain? Are you dooming your marriage relationship (present or future) by training your body to be sexually self-sufficient?

- Do you ever hear your conscience speak to you prior to committing a particular sin, but respond with a thought such as, "But God will forgive me"?

- By continually searching for any sin that dwells within your heart, do you think that, with God's help, you can learn to recognize and repent from internal drives before they blossom into external behaviors? Why or why not?

CHAPTER FIVE

True Confessions

Therefore confess your sins to one another,
and pray for one another, that you may be healed.
—JAMES 5:16

We have often heard that confession is good for the soul, and even at eight years old, my daughter, Erin, had learned this lesson well. We have had a "confession rule" in our family since the day before she started kindergarten. As I set out her new uniform, packed her backpack, and climbed in her bed for one more pep-talk about being an excellent student, I explained, "If you ever get in trouble at school, but confess when you come home, then the trouble is over. But if you get in trouble with your teacher and you don't tell Mommy about it, then the trouble is only beginning!"

Obviously those words were written permanently on her heart that night. Over the past several years, there have been times when I have had to laugh under my breath at the silly incidents she is anxious to confess when I pick her up from school. The most recent confession was, "Mommy, I accidentally saw a boy's underwear when he was swinging on the monkey bars today." Rather than laugh and discourage her confession, however, I assure her that things like that are going to happen to everybody once in a while.

As harmless as some of her "misdeeds" are, there have been other times when she committed a more serious offense and her confessions turned into a tearful prayer session in order to absolve her of her guilt. As a mother, I can always tell that something is wrong during those times when guilt is weighing her heart down. When I pick her up from school, she is usually silent, withdrawn, and somewhat emotional, especially if her little brother asks too many questions. On those days, I usually find something to occupy everyone else in the house so that Erin and I can have some time alone. Without my prompting, it usually doesn't take her long at all to spit out what is bothering her. She has learned that she will only feel better after she gets it off her chest and receives the parental assurance she hungers for.

I share this story because it is so similar to our experiences with God when we have something to confess. It seems that until we do, we feel distant from God, from others, and often from ourselves. We feel a weight on our hearts and find it hard to concentrate on anything else, for fear of how God may react. If we only remembered that God is already painfully aware of our misdeeds, we wouldn't feel the need to hide our sin (as if we could). If we could only realize how much our Heavenly Father longs for us to enter His presence, agree with Him that our sin was wrong, confess our guilt, and practice repentance, we could receive forgiveness so that our relationship with Him, with others, and with ourselves could be restored.

Many women harbor their misdeeds and carry the resulting emotional baggage around like a ball and chain, dragging it into every relationship. They become so used to dragging it behind them, everywhere they go, that they become desensitized to how much strength and effort it takes to hold the guilt inside themselves. Ladies, confession will give you such a newfound sense of freedom and release from the past that it will feel as if you have removed twenty-pound ankle weights from each leg after wearing them for years! You'll feel as if you could fly, without this added burden weighing you down! Before we discuss some of the common hindrances to confessing our sins, I want to establish two things. First, it is important to carefully select *who* you confess these issues to, and second, it is important *how* you confess them.

Selecting Your Listening Ear

When the topic of confession is brought up, perhaps it conjures up images in your mind of little rooms and Catholic priests behind black curtains. Or, at least, we imagine confession as being something we do with someone in the clergy. While that is certainly a wise choice for a listening, sympathetic ear, my personal opinion is that it is vital for women to find other women with whom to discuss these intimate issues. If you know of a female clergyperson and trust her input into your life, that is great. Other Christian women, especially those who have struggled with this issue before and overcome it, are valuable listening ears as well and have a wealth of knowledge and unique insight that they could pass along to you.

What I don't recommend, however, is airing this type of dirty laundry with any male other than your husband, clergyperson or not. I've had several women share their sad stories with me of how they confided in their pastor or youth minister, and then later felt as if their relationship had changed in a negative way. Some women say that their confidants seemed uncomfortable with the confession in light of its personal, feminine nature, thus making them feel awkward. Other women say that they could no longer face their male confidant or accept spiritual direction from him for fear of what he may be thinking of her. And sadly, some women have had the nightmarish experience of a male confidant taking advantage of the knowledge of the confessor's weaknesses and eventually pursuing a romantic relationship. That may sound shocking to many in light of the image that most people have of the clergy, but in more than a decade of ministry, I have learned one thing well—and that is that pastors are people, too. Good people, yes, but human nonetheless.

While overhearing a female voice on the radio one afternoon several years ago, I perked up when I heard her say, "In the pastoral professions, ninety percent of all extramarital affairs begin in the counseling office." As a youth minister hoping to pursue a master's degree in counseling at the time, I found that statistic quite scary. I pondered the statement, searching for explanations of such a phenomenon. The answer takes us back to the power of our words and the inappropriate nature of sharing our innermost struggles with someone of the opposite sex.

A hurting individual comes in for guidance and verbally pours emotions out on the table. The pastor/counselor invests time and energy into assisting that person through a chaotic maze. The client eventually sees progress as a result of these meetings and grows attached to the counselor, often placing him or her on a pedestal as "all-knowing and all-caring." This feeds the counselor's ego and need to be appreciated, something that perhaps hasn't been felt at home in a while. What starts out as a professional relationship evolves over time into a personal one, emotional connection already in place. The next step to physical intimacy comes all too naturally. The effect? Two shattered marriages, several confused children now struggling to cope, and an entire church community questioning, "How could this have happened?"

The more intelligent question to ask ourselves is, "How can we *avoid* this happening?" The answer is that we need women to counsel women and men to counsel men with such personal issues. If you seek professional counseling (and if this book is moving you to, I pray that you will), I strongly encourage you to seek a female counselor.

I also recommend that you not discuss your sexual past or the revelations you are now having about yourself with a male other than your husband. Although some claim to have experienced much healing in a mixed support-group setting, I personally feel as if putting male and female sex and love addicts together in a room to discuss their sexual temptations is the equivalent of holding an Alcoholics Anonymous meeting at a local bar. You might not lose control, but then again, you might. If you are not selective about those with whom you share your innermost thoughts and temptations, you could easily stumble and fall again and take someone else with you.

Divulging Too Much to Too Many

While the majority of this chapter is devoted to encouraging your confession to God, to yourself, and to another human being, let me interject balance here and say this does not require you to be an open book to anyone and everyone in your life. We are to confess to "another" human being, not "every" human being we have a relationship with. You certainly would not want to divulge too much information to too many people. Most do not know how to process or respond to such divulgence of confidences, so again, be selective in choosing your listening ear.

One woman expressed her deep sense of rejection when she shared her personal struggle with love addiction in a women's Bible study group. These ladies obviously didn't know how to handle such a personal issue and moved on quickly to the next prayer request, leaving this woman wide open but unattended to. She claimed that her humiliation would prevent her from ever returning to that group. While more care should have been extended to her, she also acknowledged that she should have exercised more caution in divulging such sensitive information to a group inexperienced in such matters. Groups that are designed to deal with such issues (support groups, self-help groups, etc.) expect to minister to you by bearing your burdens. Other groups may be blindsided by such a confession and add to your burden by responding in a counterproductive way.

Here are some other commonly asked questions about confession:

"*When should I tell my boyfriend?*" Again, the only male you should ever confess to is your husband, but your boyfriend does have a right to know about your past in general prior to becoming your fiancée or your husband. Don't make the mistake of divulging too much too early in the relationship. A plethora of sordid details will scare any guy off. Wait until the signs of eminent engagement are there (readiness for marriage, planning your futures together, discussing of goals and dreams, etc.). But by all means, let him know about your past prior to his offering or your acceptance of a marriage proposal. If you date for a few years, but decide not to get married, that is not so unusual. If you are already engaged, however, and he calls off the wedding because of your late-breaking confession, you will both suffer pain and humiliation. My advice is to take it slow (time is your friend!) and allow the gentleman to get to know who you are now before you tell him all about who you once were. Let him develop confidence in your character and your godliness. Then, when you share your personal testimony of how Christ changed your life, he will know beyond a shadow of a doubt that you are truly a new creation.

"*Should I confess to my parents?*" If you feel the need to, I certainly wouldn't advise against it. However, you do need to ask yourself, "Would my confession serve to make *them* feel better or for *me* to feel better?" If confessing to your parents would clear your conscience, but negatively affect your relationship with them, then perhaps you should not go into detail with them. But I do encourage asking forgiveness of your parents to the extent that you have wronged them. For example, I never gave my parents gory details about my sordid romances, but I did ask their forgiveness for being a rebellious teenager. I even apologized to my dad recently for not recognizing what a good father I had while I had him. His response was, "You've still got me!" Such general confessions can bring great healing in parent/child relationships.

"Do I ever need to tell my own children?" It is according to the age and maturity level of your children and what your motivation is. The same principle applies here as well. Ask yourself, "Would my confession benefit them, or only serve to make me feel better?" The mother who uses her elementary-aged child as a confidant in such matters is selfishly motivated and is exploiting her child. I would discourage airing your dirty laundry in front of your young children, as this will not help them develop a confidence in your moral character. But as your children approach adulthood, you can make such disclosures in a mature, responsible way that will benefit them. For example, the mother of a teenage son who is dating and has a steady girlfriend might feel the need to forewarn her son about the dangers and emotional baggage created by premarital sex.

My personal decision is that if my child asks me specific questions about my past, I will use discretion in order to protect their innocence, but I will not lie. As my children grow into their teenage years, if I feel that sharing a lesson learned from my past will encourage them to make wiser decisions, I will not hesitate. Hopefully they know from years of experience that their mom is a Well Woman, even if she was once a Woman at the Well.

A Wounded Healer vs. a Healing Wounder

The other aspect of confession I want to warn you about is *how* you confess your misdeeds. I've attended sex and love addicts meetings where women graphically made their confessions, detail by gory detail. While some people get bored with such rambling, others find the details quite interesting… even intriguing. Intriguing to the point that listening to her paint such a colorful picture of her sin is equivalent to watching a soap opera or reading a romance novel.

Members often leave more aroused than when they arrived.

In such cases, the confessor often unknowingly takes on the role of a "healing wounder" rather than a "wounded healer." While confession may give them some sort of release from the past, it can also easily cause others to crave, not resist, similar experiences. As necessary as confessions are in providing some closure to our pasts, we need to focus only on the sinful aspects of it and be careful to avoid the pleasurable or graphic details. By nature, our "pleasure" isn't something that demands confession. Our "sin" is what demands confession. Therefore, it might help to make a list of the internal factors operating in your heart at that moment of indulgence (selfishness, pride, fear of pain, etc.) and then, when it comes confession time, you can call a spade a spade without getting sidetracked by the graphic details.

For example, a dangerous confession sounds something like, "He was so cute and we went (here) and he said (this) and then he touched me (there)..." etc., etc. Don't defile your listener's ear with that kind of confession! A healthy confession sounds like, "I selfishly felt that I was entitled to pleasure and I was unfaithful to my commitment to avoid acting out sexually. In doing this, I crossed my own boundaries, defiled my marriage relationship, subjected myself to inner turmoil..." etc., etc. Those are the type of confessions that enable you to be a "wounded healer," helping others learn from your mistakes and providing an atmosphere of genuine repentance and restoration.

Common Hindrances to Confession

If you are uncomfortable with the whole concept of allowing another human being a glimpse into your sinful heart, ask yourself, "Why?" What is it that is holding you back from taking yet another step toward sexual wholeness? If there are things in your heart that you feel you have to hide from others, it's a good indication that you need to remove them. The pain that bringing your sin out into the open causes is often enough to inhibit you from committing that sin so easily in the future. For that reason alone, confession is worth the emotional investment. Here are some other excuses that often serve as hindrances to taking this next step toward healing:

"I am the only one struggling with this issue."—Get over that! Since the days of Adam and Eve, people have experienced temptation and often succumbed to it. There have been counselors throughout the ages treating many clients for this same issue. The reason you have always thought you were the only one is probably because you've never heard anyone else admit their similar struggles. They are thinking the same thing you are! Break the silence and give someone else the affirmation that they are not alone, either! In every church where I speak, women approach me afterward, saying, "I was a Woman at the Well, too!" They often express relief to hear that someone else has shared their pain and has had victory over such struggles. There is an immediate bond between two sisters who have walked the same path. Don't miss out on that special bond by thinking you are alone in this battle!

"No one will understand."—You are right. No one will understand until you give them a chance to understand what has been going on in your life. Your loneliness and isolation will only grow until you allow someone a glimpse into your soul. Many Christians long for such glimpses into what people are struggling with, so they can administer the salve of heaven to the hurting. God will show you who you can confide in. Simply pray for a special friend who will understand and support you so that you can go deeper in this process.

"I'll be judged."—As if you are the only one in the world with sin in your life! Jesus didn't have to hang on the cross any longer for you than He did for anyone else's sin. Anyone who judges you as a result of your sincere confession is then the one in sin! Matthew 7:1–2 says, "Do not judge, or you too will be judged. For in the same way you judge others, you will be judged, and with the measure you

use, it will be measured to you." Again, fear is the opposite of faith. In order to overcome your fear of judgement, you must have faith that God will provide a sympathetic confidant.

"*I am afraid people will spread rumors about me.*"—Chances are the rumors were flying long before you were even aware that you struggled with this issue. Other people see our hunger for attention and affection often before we recognize it ourselves. By striving for change, you are teaching others that the rumors they may have heard are no longer true, but that you are a new creation. Besides, as Christians, we should fear no other opinion than God's.

"*I don't feel that I'm acceptable to anyone else.*"—The only way to overcome this hindrance is to step out in faith and be vulnerable for once. As long as you withhold the burdens of your heart and rob others of the opportunity to accept you in spite of your shortcomings, you will never feel totally accepted or unconditionally loved. You will only feel accepted for who you think people imagine you to be. Taking off the mask and getting real with a friend may result in trust and intimacy you never thought possible.

"*I don't need to confess to be healed.*"—With no confession comes no accountability. With no accountability, it is too easy to go back to your old lifestyle when temptation strikes. Do yourself a big favor and take a vital step toward your healing process. Confess and get some accountability in your life! Ecclesiastes 4:12 says, "Though one may be overpowered, two can defend themselves. A cord of three strands is not quickly broken." You, God, and an accountability partner would make a great army in this war against your flesh.

Accountability Brings Change

In the years when I was most vulnerable to sexual temptations, I attended an accountability group regularly with some other women. I did this so I could remain vigilant over my actions, honestly share what was going on in my heart and mind with other women, and get feedback from them about how we could continue to maintain righteousness. Your healing process is very precious, and accountability relationships help us protect our investments toward becoming the women of integrity that we want to be.

I encountered a woman who claimed to have been going to a Sex and Love Addicts Anonymous group off and on for eight years. I expected that after such a long time in the program, she must be a wealth of knowledge. But as she explained what was going on in her life, it seemed as if there had been no real change in her heart at all. Although she was only having sex with her husband (her loose definition of sobriety), she continued to surf inappropriate Web sites on the Internet, converse with other men through chat rooms, rent pornographic videos, etc. I asked her if she had anyone holding her accountable to avoiding such behaviors. Sadly, she had never heard of the concept of accountability and asked what I meant. I replied by explaining the kind of relationship I've had with my accountability partners.

As I share my current temptations, I want someone to ask me next time they see me how I am doing with avoiding those pitfalls. I want to know, as I make daily choices about my thoughts, words, and actions, that I'll have to answer honestly to someone about those choices next time I see them. I want someone to challenge me and cause me to think longer and harder about my actions and my attitudes. I want someone to be honest enough with me to say things like, "Hey! The way that you were talking about (such-and-such) makes me wonder if you have some sort of hidden motives—have you searched your heart on that? Have you prayed about it?" You get the idea. Iron sharpens iron, and I want a woman who is experienced in overcoming sexual temptations to help keep me sharp. A female accountability partner can truly be "Jesus with skin on" for you, helping you to stay on the straight and narrow path. It is through having such accountability in our lives that we are able to accomplish our ultimate goal—permanent *change*, not just of behaviors, but of thoughts and attitudes as well.

Someday we will all give account to God for our list of misdeeds. Romans 14:10b–12 says,

> ...*we will all stand before God's judgment seat. It is written: "As surely as I live"' says the Lord, "every knee will bow before me; every tongue will confess to God." So then, each of us will give an account of himself to God.*

Perhaps having an accountability partner this side of heaven will spur us to have a much shorter list come that day.

No Stone to Throw

As we overcome our fear of confession, establish accountability relationships, and serve as sounding boards for other women, we must be careful to avoid judgmental attitudes. In John chapter 8, Jesus demonstrates the kind of non-judgmental attitude we should foster as He ministers to a woman caught in adultery. As the teachers of the law and the Pharisees brought this woman to Jesus, suggesting that she be stoned for such an act, Jesus was bent down writing in the sand with His finger. His response to them was, "If any one of you is without sin, let him be the first to throw a stone at her," and then He returned to writing in the sand (John 8:3–8).

As her accusers left one by one, Jesus asked her, "Woman, where are they? Has no one condemned you?"

"No one sir," she said.

"Then neither do I condemn you," Jesus declared. "Go now and leave your life of sin" (John 8: 9–11).

Two things about this passage pique my curiosity. First, what was Jesus writing with His finger in the sand? It has been speculated by some Bible scholars that perhaps He was writing the names of all the men in the land who had been a previous partner with her in adultery. Others suggest He was writing down the specific sins of those gathered there accusing this woman. Regardless of exactly what Jesus was writing, He made His point clear: Not one of us is without sin; therefore, not one of us can condemn our brother or sister. Only God alone is worthy of judging sin.

The other mind-boggling point about this passage of Scripture is that this woman was caught *in the act* of adultery. In other words, there was no question about her guilt. Yet, Jesus chose not to follow the letter of the law and carry out justice. He reached beyond justice to mercy. His desire was not to condemn her, but to love her into a right relationship with God once again. He bid her to go and leave her life of sin. Like only Jesus can, He freed her (and us) for joyful obedience. I am sure that such an encounter with Jesus inspired this woman to obey His command, not out of a sense of obligation, but out of loving response to His mercy. In John 14:15, Jesus says, "If you love Me, you will obey what I command." As we deepen our love relationship with Christ, we realize that we no longer *have* to obey. Because of His love, His grace, and His mercy, we *want* to obey.

As you confess your sin to God, to yourself, and to a trusted confidant, may you also be freed for joyful obedience.

 QUESTIONS FOR INTROSPECTION:

• Prior to reading this chapter, what was your reaction to the need to confess your sin to another human being?

- What hindrances to confession listed in this chapter could you identify with?

- How can these hindrances be overcome in your mind?

- Who in your life do you envision as a compassionate yet convicting accountability partner?

- What do you fear most about having real accountability in your life?

- What do you think would be the greatest benefit of having such an accountability relationship?

- Is Christ's unconditional love, grace and mercy enough to free you for joyful obedience? Why or why not?

CHAPTER SIX

Removing the Scarlet Letter

"Remain in me, and I will remain in you.
No branch can bear fruit by itself; it must remain in the vine.
Neither can you bear fruit unless you remain in me."
—JOHN 15:4

While being able to recognize our sinful reflection in the mirror is one of the most difficult stretches of the journey toward sexual wholeness (one that many women never successfully complete), it is still only the beginning. The road ahead has many twists and turns, but let us not forget the destination we are pressing toward: *Christ-likeness.* That is our goal. And we need a road map and a tour guide to help us arrive safely at that destination. Our road map? The Bible. God's holy Word is complete with directions for safe travel toward genuine love, joy, peace, patience, kindness, goodness, faithfulness, gentleness, and self-control. Our tour guide? The Holy Spirit, who is in essence Christ Himself. Remember your parents warning you, "You are what your friends are! Choose your friends wisely!"? How true! Proverbs 13:20 says, "He who walks with the wise grows wise, but a companion of fools suffers harm." What better companion on this journey toward Christ-likeness than the Holy Spirit—Christ dwelling within us?

Behavior vs. Character

As we continue this journey together, let us pause here for revelation and an even greater understanding of how important our character is, as well as to examine the difference between our behavior and our character. You see, Christ doesn't look at you or your future based on your past. He isn't concerned with what you have done before. He died to forgive all of those things, and they have been removed as far as the east is from the west (Psalm 103:12). No, Christ is concerned about your character... and a Christ-like character can only come from an intimate relationship with Christ Himself, not from simply modifying our behavior.

I've learned this lesson well over the past several years, because I tried many of the "behavior modification" techniques we've learned about. I went to church; I had accountability friendships; I changed how I dressed, etc., etc. I even went for many years without acting out sexually. Just as you have heard the term "dry drunk" to describe someone who is no longer drinking, but is still an alcoholic nonetheless, my addiction was only lying dormant and the fear of "relapsing" back into old patterns haunted me.

Even though I was outwardly behaving with more Christ-likeness than ever before, my inward character was still not a direct reflection of Him. I was painfully aware that there were still passions and desires flooding my heart and mind, and that even though I had managed to change my outward behavior, I never felt as if *I* had been changed.

In *False Intimacy: Understanding the Struggle of Sexual Addiction,* Dr. Harry Schaumburg writes:

> Receiving restorative healing is much more than simply renewing your own efforts to do what is right. It is much more than just choosing to stop your addictive behaviors. Without God's help, you can modify your behaviors through willpower,

perhaps even stopping them for a long period of time. But you'll continue to wrestle with internal struggles with no hope of conquering them. Sin is too strong to overcome on your own. You must pursue God on His terms, in brokenness and humility, facing the sinful condition of your heart and inviting God to begin healing you.[1]

The Point of No Return

One of the turning points in my journey toward sexual wholeness occurred in 1993 while on my *Walk to Emmaus*, a seventy-two-hour women's spiritual retreat. A female pastor (I'll call her "Beverly") gave a personal testimony of how God had called her into ordained ministry in her early forties. She wrestled with God about this, arguing that she was a woman, that she had been sexually promiscuous in the past, and that she was divorced, convinced that these strikes disqualified her from ministry. "But God!" she had said, "Pastors aren't usually divorced women with a past like mine!" Then she was reminded about the impact the original Woman at the Well had when she went back to Samaria to give testimony about her life-changing encounter with Jesus. John 4:39–42 reads,

> *Many of the Samaritans from that town believed in Him because of the woman's testimony, "He told me everything I ever did." So when the Samaritans came to Him, they urged Him to stay with them, and He stayed two days. And because of His words many more became believers. They said to the woman, "We no longer believe just because of what you said; now we have heard for ourselves and we know that this man really is the Savior of the world."*

God asked her, "Have *you* had a life-changing encounter with Me, Beverly? Won't you give testimony to what I've done in your life? Won't you lead My lost sheep back home to Me?"

I was so broken by hearing her testimony, because it paralleled mine so closely, and I knew that the Lord had the both of us on the same weekend for a reason. At the time, I was a pre-med student and was serving as a volunteer youth worker in our church. I sensed that God wanted me to give up my own dreams of becoming a doctor and lead His young sheep back into His fold by becoming a professional youth minister. I had the same excuses—"But God! I messed up my teenage years so badly! How do you expect me to lead other teenagers? I'm no role model! You don't know *what* you are asking or *who* you are asking it of!" Looking back, I can't believe I questioned God's sanity, but that is in essence what I was doing. "God must be crazy to ask me to be a youth minister!" I thought. And I was right. God *was* crazy. He was crazy about *me*! And He was crazy about teenagers. And He wanted me to testify to how He had changed my life, so that others would know He wants to change their lives, too.

Removing the Scarlet Letter

After Beverly's talk, I approached her, sobbing, and asked if I could speak with her alone for a few moments. We went outside and sat underneath a towering oak tree, and I poured my emotional baggage out on the ground. I asked her, "How do I answer this call to ministry? Where do I begin to pick up the pieces and move on to what God has for me to do?"

Beverly responded, "You begin by taking the scarlet letter off of your chest so that God can use you!" (referring to Nathaniel Hawthorn's classic novel, *The Scarlet Letter*, in which Hester Prynne was forced by the townspeople to wear a scarlet letter "A" on her chest as a reminder that she was an "Adulteress.") She went on to explain that as I was spilling my guts, I still talked as if all of those misdeeds were still a part of who I was. I was still wearing my scarlet letter, and I lived in fear of going back to my old lifestyle. I thought I was still an adulteress. I knew I wasn't actively committing adultery anymore, but I had never understood that having Christ as my Savior meant that I was justified (it was "just-if-I'd" never done those things!). This conversation was a major part of my sanctification process—the process where we become more and more Christ-like because we gain more and more of an understanding of who Christ is and who we are in Christ.

But many of us have never changed our labels based on who we are in Christ. We often continue to view ourselves through the labels that have been cast upon us by others. Women still feel the sting of harsh words from their past, such as "slut," "whore," etc. Unknowingly, those labels have often served as a self-fulfilling prophecy. Because we believe people view us as "sluts," we've often acted like sluts. But God views you as His precious beloved. It is time to take the scarlet letter off of your sweater and start acting like His precious beloved!

As I ventured further into God's will and became a youth minister, I witnessed God using my personal testimony to bring great glory to Himself. Seeing young people turn their lives over to God in spite of the mistakes they had made or the sin they had committed fueled my fire to continue being real with people about how God had pursued me and wooed me into an intimate love relationship with Him.

From Lemons to Lemonade

Isn't it funny how God takes our lemons (our sour mistakes) and then turns them into such sweet lemonade that whets the appetite of others to know more about God? Let's talk about that process for a moment. Who else but God can take the bitterness of sin, add drops of His grace and mercy, and create such a sweet story out of it? If you have lots of lemons in your life, consider this process that God longs to perform: *What must be done to lemons to make lemonade?*

First, they must be picked. God must take the lemons from you. Better yet, you must hand them over. You must let go and let God take away your sin—all sin. Forget holding on to any unhealthy relationships. Forget holding on to bitterness and anger toward those who have wronged you. Forget holding on to your pride, and humbly admit you have these lemons and that there is nothing that you can do by yourself that will make them anything but sour!

Next, they must be cut open. In other words, our hearts must be circumcised. We must agree with the ugliness of our sin, acknowledge how it has only served to distance us from God and His perfect will for our lives, and come broken before the Lord. We must stop trying to fix ourselves by simply modifying our behavior. We must be entirely ready to have God remove all these defects of character.

The third step in this process is that the lemons must be squeezed to separate the good stuff (the juice) from the bad stuff (the pulp). God longs to capture any Christ-likeness that you already possess and the spiritual gifts He has placed inside of you. But in order to bring it to perfection, He must remove it from the sin that absorbs the good and makes it invisible to others. Think about it. If you had never seen or heard of a lemon when you first cut one open, you wouldn't recognize that there was good juice flowing through the fibers of the pulp, because all you would see is pulp. The same is true with our lives. Others do not see the Christ-likeness or spiritual gifts that are already inside of us, because it is hidden by the obvious sin in our lives. By applying pressure through circumstances, relationships, or whatever means He chooses, God separates us from our sin. This sanctification process is not about us changing our behavior, it is about God "squeezing out" our character flaws. By allowing God to perfect our character, our behavior will automatically be changed as a result.

The last step in the process is adding something to the lemon juice in order to transform it into sweet lemonade. First, God adds Living Water through your personal relationship with Christ. Then,

He adds enough grace and mercy to transform your life into a powerful testimony with the ability to lead others to want to quench their thirst for God through a similar transformation experience.

One final note about this lemonade that God is going to make out of your lemons—what must be done to keep lemonade from separating, where the good part settles at the bottom of the pitcher where no one can taste it anymore and the rest gets all watered down? It must be stirred regularly. We must make sure and ask the Holy Spirit to keep our hearts and our spirits stirred up for God and for the people He loves, so that our testimony never loses its sweetness!

God Uses Broken Vessels

Mary Magdalene is a prime example from Scripture about a life changed by the power of Jesus. She was possessed by seven demons when she met Jesus. After her encounter with Him, she was an incredible testimony about how Jesus could drive out any evil and transform a bitter life into unsurpassed sweetness. Mary followed Jesus from Galilee, helping Him spread the good news of God's love for the people. She took care of Jesus' personal needs, helping support Him with her own money. She was true to Jesus until the end and remained with Him at Golgotha, weeping desperately as the soldiers crucified her Lord.

Regardless of Mary Magdalene's past, Jesus obviously trusted her immensely. I believe this because Scripture tells us that when Jesus arose from the dead, the first person He appeared to was Mary Magdalene (John 20:10–18). In fact, Jesus charged her with delivering the news to the disciples that He had, in fact, risen from the dead (John 20:17). Obviously people had witnessed such an incredible change in her life that there would be no mistaking Mary as still being possessed by demons when she delivered such unusual news. Jesus knew she would be a trustworthy messenger and her testimony would be considered valid by those who knew her.

Mary Magdalene was a broken vessel, which is the only kind of vessel God can use. He cannot use a vessel that holds what God has poured in and keeps it inside. He uses those of us who are broken, for we allow God's grace and mercy to flow through our cracks onto dry and thirsty ground and into other vessels!

Have you heard the old folk tale about the broken clay jar? A young boy in a tribal village had the responsibility of bringing water from the spring to his family's hut each day. He carried a pole horizontally on his back with a clay water jar tied to each end of the pole. But one of the clay jars had a crack in it and leaked water all the way from the spring to the hut. One day, the clay jar sadly asked the boy, "Why do you continue to use me when I fail to carry all of your water back to your hut? Why have you not replaced me with another clay jar?" The boy smiled at the jar and pointed to the roadside where beautiful flowers lined the path and brought glorious color and sweet fragrance to the tribe's drab world. He replied, "I use your brokenness to bring joy and happiness to my people." Stop fretting over your brokenness and start watching for beauty to bloom as a result of God flowing through you.

God's Faithfulness to Unfaithful People

I have learned to embrace my own brokenness and have come to understand that my imperfections make God's perfection all that much more sought after in my own life. A vivid illustration that reminds me of how God will always be faithful to me, even when I have not been faithful to Him, is the story of Hosea and Gomer (from the Book of Hosea in the Old Testament—a must-read for Women at the Well!). Hosea is instructed by God to take a wife, not of noble character, but of harlotry. Their marriage was to be a symbol of the relationship between God and His people, the Israelites. Even though they committed spiritual adultery, pursuing pagan deities as "lovers" in the place of God, God's love for

Israel never wavered and He held fast to His part of the covenant established with them. As a prostitute, Gomer was unfaithful to her husband time and time again, pursuing other lovers and turning her face from their marriage vows. But God told Hosea to reconcile with his wife each time, for it was an illustration of how He would never refuse to reconcile with Israel. Regardless of how unfaithful they were to God, God would always be faithful to them, pursuing them with His redeeming love and drawing them back into a right relationship with Him.

This story is also a painful reminder of how we have not only committed sexual adultery by engaging in sex before marriage, but also spiritual adultery by being unfaithful to the Lover of our soul. Have you ever thought about the fact that when you spend more time daydreaming about that handsome guy you met recently than about the God that created you, you are committing spiritual adultery? When you spend more time pursuing an intimate relationship with an earthly man than you do an intimate relationship with your Heavenly Father, you are being unfaithful to Him. When the greater longing in your heart is for a husband rather than for Jesus, it breaks His heart, for you are His bride, and He is your groom.

Spiritual adultery can also be referred to as "idolatry." Idolatry is what prompted the first two of the Ten Commandments. Exodus 20:3–6 says,

You shall have no other gods before Me. You shall not make for yourself an idol in the form of anything in the heaven above or on the earth beneath or in the waters below. You shall not bow down to them or worship them; for I, the Lord your God, am a jealous God, punishing the children for the sin of the fathers to the third and fourth generation of those who hate Me, but showing love to a thousand generations of those who love Me and keep My commandments.

Making an "Idol" Out of Love

When we think of idolatry, we think of a golden calf or a statue of some sort. But haven't we often made idols of men, bowing down to worship them in our hearts each time we craved their attention? We also long for a relationship with a man who will become totally obsessed with our beauty, our wit, and our charm, but beware if and when this happens. Why? Because if a man always has you on his mind, he is "idolizing" you, and that makes you a prime target for God's wrath. One motto I have written in permanent ink on my brain is, "God is determined to make bitter anything that is treasured above Him!" I do not want to be treasured above God in any relationship and I will not pursue any earthly relationship more avidly than I pursue my relationship with the Lord, or else I know it is doomed to become bitter.

Thankfully, relationships that took first place in my heart in the past did, in fact, turn bitter; the true fulfillment that I was searching for has finally been found as a result of God taking His rightful first place in my heart. He is so good to look beyond our immediate wants to give us what we genuinely need.

Breathing the Right Kind of Air

A witty friend shared a clever analogy with me once. She said, "Gee, being addicted to love is like being addicted to air! You have to have it, but you have to learn how to make sure you are breathing the right kind of air, and not carbon monoxide or something!"

It is true; feeling loved is vital to life. But expecting to get all the love we need from a relationship with a man is like trying to breathe carbon monoxide—we are doomed to eventually die, because his love will never be enough to sustain us. Only God's love is pure enough to sustain us throughout life.

What kind of air are *you* breathing? Are you choking on the exhaust fumes from some polluted relationship, or are you inhaling the sweet fragrance of Jesus' everlasting love? Just as we have craved fresh air since the doctor slapped our bare behinds to make us breathe for the first time, we also crave the pure, unconditional love of our Creator. Take a few moments today to breathe deeply and savor the life-giving air. Savor the lavish love of the Life-Giver, who fills not just our lungs, but our hearts as well.

QUESTIONS FOR INTROSPECTION:

• Are you still wearing a scarlet letter on your sweater? Do you still see yourself as an "adulteress?"

• What are some of the lemons (bitter mistakes) you have picked in your life?

• What kind of lemonade (sweetness) do you think God could make out of those lemons if you allowed Him to?

- What "behavior modification" attempts have you made in the past?

- What are the "character flaws" that have continued to drive your behavior in the past?

- Are you ready to have God search your heart and remove those character flaws? Why or why not?

- Prior to this journey, what did you think "adultery" and "idolatry" meant?

- In what ways have you violated these commandments?

- In what ways has God been faithful to you in spite of your unfaithfulness?

- How can you show your appreciation for such an incomparably devoted love?

CHAPTER SEVEN

The Perfecting Process

"Truly, truly, I say to you, unless one is born anew,
he cannot see the kingdom of God...
that which is born of the flesh is flesh, and that
which is born of the Spirit is Spirit."
—JOHN 3:3–6

Perfecting us? Truly changing us from the inside out? Wow! Seems like such a tall order, doesn't it? We've often wondered if it is even a real possibility, as often as we have failed at permanently modifying our behavior. But being perfected is not accomplished by our own attempts at modifying our behavior. It is accomplished by allowing the Holy Spirit entrance into our hearts to cleanse even the most subconscious of our character flaws, so that we can operate out of His perfect righteousness rather than out of our sinful nature. In order for you to gain a clearer understanding of how this process works, let's briefly examine Christ's restoration of humans after the Fall of Man (when Adam and Eve committed the first sin) and the work of the Holy Spirit. Entire books have been written on this topic, so we can't possibly begin to do it justice here; but let's at least draw the big picture.

Back to the Beginning

The Adam from Genesis with whom we are all familiar is referred to as "the first Adam," because he was the first human that God created and gave commands to. Jesus Christ is often called "the last Adam," because His redemptive work on the cross ended the vicious cycle of humans trying to merely obey God's commands through "living by the law." As Adam and every human being after him discovered, perfect obedience was not humanly possible. That is, until God became human Himself.

Before Christ came to fulfill the "New Covenant," prophesied about throughout the Old Testament, the central theme of Scripture was God calling a select group of people (the Israelites) to be His own and to live by the laws He established through Moses. These laws were designed so that the people could be holy (or "set apart") from their wicked culture, because God is holy. But in their sinful human nature, the Israelites failed time and time again to be an obedient people. God performed miraculous signs and wonders to prove Himself as their almighty deliverer and provider, and patiently sought their trust and obedience. He parted the Red Sea in order to save them from Pharoah's army. He provided manna, quail and water for each day's needs while they wandered forty years in the desert. He gave Israel the ability to conquer much larger armies in order to take possession of the land God had promised them on oath through their forefathers Abraham, Isaac, and Jacob. He was a covenant-keeping God, but Israel was a covenant-breaking people.

However, God had a divine plan in mind to redeem His people and to bring them to perfection. First, He would send a part of Himself to earth, in the form of a man, in order to give them a living example of perfect obedience to these laws. This man would live not by the letter of the law, being legalistic and "holier-than-thou" in His views, as the Pharisees and teachers of the law were. He would live by the spirit of the law, always being obedient to the Law-maker and living in servitude to the people whom the laws were created to guide. Then God would demonstrate to the entire world His unparalleled love for them, by placing all of their (and our) sins (past, present, and future) on the shoulders of His own Son.

Believers in the Old Testament slaughtered an innocent lamb without blemish as a sacrifice for the remission of their sins. But Jesus Christ, the Lamb of God, would serve as the ultimate sacrifice for all the sin of mankind, putting an end to our slavery and bondage to our fleshly ways. Finally, God would send still another part of Himself to earth in the form of the Holy Spirit. This time, He would live not on the earth, but in our hearts, so that we could also be internally driven to live by the spirit of the law.

When Jesus foretold His eminent death to His disciples, they became distraught at the idea of no longer having Him in their presence to teach and to guide them. But Jesus assured them that God's plan was certainly in their best interest. Understand that while Jesus was in the flesh here on earth, He had all of the limitations of being human. He could only teach, heal and minister to others as He personally encountered them (or through His appointed agents, such as the disciples, or the Centurion in Matthew 8).

Upon His death, resurrection, and ascension into heaven, Jesus would send the Holy Spirit to dwell in the hearts of all believers and be unlimited in His ability to guide every heart who would seek to follow Him. The disciples were promised this *paraclete* (translated as *comforter, helper, advocate*) in John 14:15–20:

> *If you love me, you will obey what I command. And I will ask the Father, and He will give you another Counselor to be with you forever—the Spirit of truth. The world cannot accept Him, because it neither sees Him nor knows Him. But you know Him, for He lives with you and will be in you. I will*

not leave you as orphans; I will come to you. Before long, the world will not see me anymore, but you will see me. Because I live, you also will live. On that day you will realize that I am in my Father, and you are in me, and I am in you.

God, in the form of the Holy Spirit, could live anywhere He chooses, and He chooses to live *in you*. We are a *part* of the Holy Trinity (God the Father, God the Son, and God the Holy Spirit) when we have the Holy Spirit residing *in* us. That makes us *partners* with God!

How Well Do You Know Your Partner?

It is amazing to me how little Christians actually know about this Partner that lives within us and possesses the ability to completely transform lives. In his book, *The Biblical Basis of Christian Counseling for People Helpers*, Gary Collins gives insight into most people's impression of the Holy Spirit through his own personal revelation:

> When I was growing up in Canada, I attended a church where missions were emphasized, where the youth programs were good, and where the Bible was taught. That church was an island of stability for me during some difficult teenage years, but in thinking back, I can't remember anybody ever talking about the Holy Spirit.
>
> Across town, a large Pentecostal congregation worshiped enthusiastically and the church leaders talked often about the Holy Spirit. In our church, we saw these brothers and sisters as fellow believers, but we tended to think that their worship was too emotional so we didn't get together with them very often. In retrospect, I think my early training left the impression that the Holy Spirit was for hand-clapping charismatics but not of much relevance for people like me.
>
> Nothing could be further from the truth. Like God the

Father and Jesus Christ the Son, the Holy Spirit is God. He is alive, in the world today, living within each believer (Romans 8:9,11), and one person of the Trinity who has come to be with us forever (John 14:16,26; 15:26; 16:7).[1]

What does all this mean? It means that the same Spirit that resided in Jesus and enabled Him to live a sinless life now resides in us! We have Christ within us! Jesus is not some dead guy who went to heaven and is waiting for you to get there, too. He is inside your very soul, in the form of the Holy Spirit, longing for you to take your eyes off of your self and the pleasures of this world long enough to tune in to all that He has to reveal to you. Christ longs to cleanse you of your past, wipe away your guilt and shame, restore your dignity and self-esteem, and lead you to become the Well Woman you were created to be. He is the Lifter of our heads and the Lover of our souls, and He longs for us to seek a face-to-face connection with Him, see our precious reflection in His eyes, and hear His tender voice as He whispers, *"I love you more than you could ever comprehend. All that you are looking for, you will only find in Me. Abide in Me and I will abide in you, fulfilling your every need and perfecting you."*

The Perfect Example from Proverbs

Most Women at the Well suffer from a low opinion of themselves. That is why they are constantly reaching out for some affirmation—because they have no affirmation within themselves to draw from. They don't like themselves. They don't measure up. They are not as perfect as they think they should be. They look for the attention of a man for assurance that they are attractive and acceptable, but that attention sucks them in like a whirling drain and they wind up "in the pipes" of misery before long. They beat themselves up because they went too far. So now they feel worse than they did before they had the guy's attention in the first place. What do they eventually do to make themselves feel better? You guessed it—next target. Whether you hit or miss with a guy, it seems to damage your self-esteem either way. Where can we get a positive self-esteem? From seeing ourselves through the eyes of our Creator and trying to excel at what He created us to be.

I believe that was the secret of the Proverbs 31 Woman. She saw herself as a woman on a mission to be a loyal wife, a loving mother, an productive worker, a shrewd businesswoman, a charitable caretaker, and a lover of her Lord. Let's look at her in detail:

A wife of noble character who can find? She is worth far more than rubies. Her husband has full confidence in her and lacks nothing of value. She brings him good, not harm, all the days of her life. She selects wool and flax and works with eager hands. She is like the merchant ships, bringing her food from afar. She gets up while it is still dark; she provides food for her family and portions for her servant girls. She considers a field and buys it; out of her earnings she plants a vineyard. She sets about her work vigorously; her arms are strong for her tasks. She sees that her trading is profitable, and her lamp does not go out at night. In her hand she holds the distaff and grasps the spindle with her fingers. She opens her arms to the poor and extends her hands to the needy. When it snows, she has no fear for her household; for all of them are clothed in scarlet. She makes coverings for her bed; she is clothed in fine linen and purple. Her husband is respected at the city gate, where he takes his seat among the elders of the land. She makes linen garments and sells them, and supplies the merchants with sashes. She is clothed with strength and dignity; she can laugh at the days to come. She speaks with wisdom, and faithful instruction is on her tongue. She watches over the affairs of her household and does not eat the bread of idleness. Her children

arise and call her blessed; her husband also, and he praises her:
"Many women do noble things, but you surpass them all."
Charm is deceptive, and beauty is fleeting; but a woman who
fears the Lord is to be praised. Give her the reward she has
earned, and let her works bring her praise at the city gate
(Proverbs 31:10–31).

Who Can Live Up To That?

While some women are inspired and encouraged by reading this passage of Scripture, I've heard women complain that there is no way they can live up to that intimidating woman, as if she were someone's fantasy of the perfect wife and mother. Regardless of your past, regardless of what has been done to you, you were still created to be a woman of noble character. While arriving at true perfection may not be possible this side of heaven, progress toward perfection certainly is.

Begin by allowing the Holy Spirit to guide your thoughts, words, and activities each day. As Proverbs 31 women, we are to be trustworthy servants of God, of our husbands, and of our children. We are to be good stewards of our time, talents, and resources, and examples to those around us. This Scripture does not seek to put a guilt trip on you for not being able to live up to this standard. It is encouragement to try to bring honor to God, to your family and friends, and as a result, to yourself. It is to show you how to become a Well Woman instead of a Woman at the Well.

Refiner's Fire

It may seem like a long stretch going from a Woman at the Well to a Well Woman, but God has a way of refining us to where only the good remains. Are you aware of what the process of "refining" entails?

In order to remove all of the impurities from gold, leaving behind only the absolute purest of substance, a refining process is necessary. This involves grinding the gold into powder and mixing it with a substance called flux. As this mixture is melted in a blazing furnace, the purest of gold sinks to the bottom and the impurities rise to the top. Then the refiner can take an instrument and rake the impurities off of the top (kind of like skimming the fat off of the top of a pot of soup). This process is repeated, over and over, until impurities have all been removed and the gold is completely pure. The refiner knows of the gold's purity when he can clearly see his reflection.

As God begins the refining process in us, our impurities float to the surface and He gently skims them off, leaving only the purest of character behind. He can see more and more of His own image shining through us as this refining continues throughout our lives. As you have read this book, I'm sure you have felt the heat of the Holy Spirit revealing and removing many impurities from you. Doesn't the purity of what the Holy Spirit leaves behind make the heat worth bearing? Doesn't the thought of Christ being reflected more clearly in your life make the pain of the refining process worthwhile?

Paul's Perfection Process

The apostle Paul went through such a process. Just as going from a Woman at the Well to a Well Woman isn't an overnight transformation, but a process, Paul did not go from being a Christian-hating murderer to one of the greatest missionaries for Christ overnight. The story of Paul (previously named Saul) begins to unfold in Acts chapter 9. It begins, "Meanwhile, Saul was still breathing out murderous threats against the Lord's disciples..." and he was on his way to Damascus to imprison and torture other Christians (he had already given approval to the stoning death of

Stephen). Prior to reaching his destination, Saul was stricken blind with a bright light from heaven. The Lord asked him, in an audible voice, "Saul, Saul, why do you persecute Me?" He instructed Saul to continue to the city, and that a man named Ananias would come to him to restore his sight. When Ananias was told by the Lord to go to Saul, he feared for his life, for he knew Saul's reputation. But the Lord said, "Go! This man is My chosen instrument to carry My name before the Gentiles and their kings and before the people of Israel..." (Acts 9:15).

Here is another prime example of how God doesn't call the equipped; *He equips the called.* He doesn't wait until Saul straightens up. He doesn't hide and watch how Saul progresses in his faith. God knows without a doubt that He has the power to transform Saul's life, and *that* He does! But not immediately. Oh, sure—it didn't take God long to reveal Himself to Saul (called Paul after his conversion) and make a believer out of him, but my guess is that Paul's character probably had to be developed prior to answering this tremendous call on his life. It is estimated that eleven years passed from the time of his conversion until God sent him out on his first missionary journey. So, the next time you get impatient with God, remember Paul. Eleven years is quite a transformation period!

Press On, Paul!

As the writer of the majority of the New Testament, Paul has many other valuable lessons to teach us. He may not have been a Woman at the Well, but he certainly had a colorful past that he wasn't very proud of. Yet, in spite of his previous unrighteousness, Paul claims in Philippians 3:12–14:

> *I press on to take hold of that for which Christ Jesus took hold of me. Brothers, I do not consider myself yet to have taken hold*

of it. But one thing I do: Forgetting what is behind and straining toward what is ahead, I press on toward the goal to win the prize for which God has called me heavenward in Christ Jesus.

Are you ready to forget what is behind you and strain toward what is ahead? Are you prepared to press on toward your goal of being a Well Woman? The more of yourself that you invest in this process, the more returning to your previous lifestyle will seem unimaginable. A life of emotional neediness pales in comparison to confidently remaining in relationship with Jesus. Of course, that is not to say you won't have your moments of temptation!

Temptation Strikes Again and Again

One of Satan's favorite tools is to discourage and frustrate believers into thinking, "I might as well go through with it, since I'm already guilty of having *those kind* of thoughts anyway." That is *false* guilt! The only thing you are guilty of is being human! The day you stop experiencing temptation is the day you die! Remember that temptation is not a sin in and of itself! In Hebrews 4:15, we read how Jesus "was tempted in every way, just as we are—yet was without sin." Since Jesus was tempted, yet still sinless, the only conclusion to draw from that passage is that experiencing temptation is not a sin.

I love the saying, "You can't keep a bird from flying over your head, but you can keep him from building a nest in your hair!" In other words, as a human being, you can't stop random thoughts entering into your brain. The question is, what are you going to do with them? Are you going to dwell on them and entertain them, or are you going to cast them out and distract your thoughts back to something pure? Paul tells us, in Philippians 4:8, "Whatever is true, whatever is noble, whatever is right, whatever is pure, whatever is lovely, whatever is admirable—if anything is excellent or praise-worthy—think about such things."

As much of a spiritual giant as Paul was, he obviously had similar struggles with temptation. In 2 Corinthians 2:7–10, he writes,

> *To keep me from becoming conceited because of these surpassingly great revelations, there was given me a thorn in my flesh, a messenger of Satan, to torment me. Three times I pleaded with the Lord to take it away from me. But he said to me, "My grace is sufficient for you, for my power is made perfect in weakness." Therefore I will boast all the more gladly about my weaknesses, so that Christ's power may rest on me. That is why, for Christ's sake, I delight in weaknesses, in insults, in hardships, in persecutions, in difficulties. For when I am weak, then I am strong.*

So, if you have a thorn in your flesh, or when you are facing temptation, rejoice that Satan has counted you a worthy target. He wouldn't bother to pursue someone who poses no threat to him. Then remind yourself that God's grace is sufficient for you, too. When you are humanly weak, His spiritual strength will inspire you to keep on keeping on!

Perfectly Single?

Another lesson that we can learn from Paul is that you can live a complete life and accomplish great things, even if you never marry. He writes in 1 Corinthians 7:32–35:

> *I would like you to be free from concern. An unmarried man is concerned about the Lord's affairs—how he can please the Lord. But a married man is concerned about the affairs of this world—how he can please his wife—and his interests are divided. An unmarried woman or virgin is concerned about*

the Lord's affairs: Her aim is to be devoted to the Lord in both
body and spirit. But a married woman is concerned about the
affairs of this world—how she can please her husband. I am
saying this for your own good, not to restrict you, but that you
may live in a right way in undivided devotion to the Lord.

Single? Forever? "No way!" you say? Well, only eighty percent of
women ever marry. That leaves a one-in-five chance that you won't
have an earthly husband. These odds shouldn't create a "race to find
my own husband because I don't want to be an old maid" mentality. If remaining single is God's perfect will for your life, don't
you think He knows what is best for you? If you remain single, you
can bet it is because God knows you would be miserable in a marriage. Don't look at singleness as punishment. Look at it as protection from relational misery and an incredible opportunity to
wholeheartedly serve others in the name of Christ, without worldly
affairs to distract you. Do you love and trust God enough to say,
"You are husband enough for me! I trust that only You know what is
best for me and I accept Your perfect will for my life, regardless of
whether it includes a man or not!"?

Stop anxiously anticipating a man that may or may not ever
come along, and start living in the here and now, making the most
of each day and enjoying life to its fullest. Invest in the relationships you do have with your family, your friends, your neighbors,
your church, your community, and your world. Invest in your
career or your ministry, or whatever gives you personal fulfillment
and a sense of significance in this world. Rather than always
looking for that morsel of attention from a man, tend to your own
emotional needs through a deeper relationship with the only One
who can truly satisfy those needs in the first place.

The season of singleness is a season to be cherished in your
life. If the season lingers, so should the preciousness of it. If the
season eventually proves temporary, at least you can look back on

it with a smile. In *The Lady, Her Lover, and Her Lord*, Bishop T.D. Jakes writes:

> Most people spend no time entertaining themselves. They only entertain others. They never plan an evening for themselves. They endure their time alone as if they had been exiled to solitary confinement. But it is the single woman who has the time to develop true spirituality. She is not encumbered with the concerns of children or mate. She has the time to strengthen herself on several different levels. She has the time to strengthen her economy, her spirituality, and her personality. Each area needs to be strengthened so that she can clearly discern, when offers come, whether she is in love or in need.[2]

Oh, I pray that you never accept a marriage proposal out of need. No marriage at all is far better than a marriage with the wrong person. 'Tis more desirable to be a happy single woman than a miserable wife.

Mastering Marriage

Should marriage be a part of your divine destiny, remind yourself that one of the keys to mastering marriage is to first master singleness. While the phrase, "You complete me!" sounded smooth coming from Tom Cruise in the movie *Jerry McGuire*, know that the philosophy of needing a mate to complete you is a bunch of garbage. A complete marriage is not the union of two incomplete people. It is the union of two people who are already complete. If you are not whole enough to know what your needs are and how to satisfy them, how do you expect to ever teach a husband how to satisfy you? Even though I'm sure husbands wished that they did, wives do not come with instruction manuals. Recognizing, communicating, and satisfying each other's needs is a lifelong process in a marriage relationship, and it is a huge part of what makes your journey through life together so fun. You can begin this process even now by recognizing your own neediness and by allowing the Maker of those emotional needs to personally satisfy them.

How do you discover completion? How do we get from brokenness to wholeness? Let's turn once again to Bishop T.D. Jakes' words in *The Lady, Her Lover, and Her Lord,* for he states it far more eloquently than I ever could:

> The goal is ultimately a state of wholeness. That wholeness cannot be reached if you are not divorced from your past and prepared for your future. So let's take it step by step, one day at a time, and watch God give you the grace to make changes and institute goals for your future.
>
> Your assignment at this point is quite simple. You have three Ps that you are to start with. They are prayer, praise, and pampering. Pray for strength because you know that He gives might to those who have none. Praise God for your survival because you know that it is by His mercy that you are still here. Pamper for solace. It is through pampering yourself that you find renewal and comfort against the tragedies of life. You could do all of these practices at the same time. Light a candle in the bathroom, play some soft notes, and slip into a hot tub with scented bath beads. Lie in the water and raise your hands in the air and praise the God that blessed you to be alive. Pray about the things that would normally worry you. Refuse to spend the evening worrying about things over which you have no control. Instead, lather up and relax—this is your time of pampering![3]

Yes, to everything there is a season, a time for every purpose under heaven (Ecclesiastes 3:1). Savor this time of your life. The Lord has ordained this to be a season of self-awareness, spiritual growth, and positive change. Enter into the cocoon of transformation with a glad heart, knowing that the Holy Spirit is perfecting your character and giving you beauty for your ashes. Allow Him to change you from the inside out, and you will emerge in His perfect timing with brilliant wings of the purest gold, reflecting the incredible beauty of your Lord.

 QUESTIONS FOR INTROSPECTION:

- Reminding yourself of John 14:15, "If you love Me, you will obey what I command," what specifically are some of the things God has commanded you to do? Is your level of obedience a direct reflection of your love?

- What has your impression of the Holy Spirit been in the past?

- How has this chapter changed that impression?

- In reading Proverbs 31, what are the traits of the wife of noble character that you feel God has blessed you with already?

- What are the specific character traits that you admire and desire for God to develop in you?

- What are the impure character traits that you want God to refine in you?

- Has Satan tried his "false guilt" strategy with you? How will you avoid falling into that trap?

- Do you trust God enough to know that His will for your life is perfect, whether it includes a husband or not?

- What can you do to fulfill your assignment of prayer, praise and pampering? How can you and the Lord tend to your own emotional, mental, and spiritual needs together, without the involvement of a man in this season of your life?

CHAPTER EIGHT

Forgive Us Our Trespasses

"So if you are offering a gift at the altar, and there remember
that your brother has something against you, leave your gift
there before the altar and go; first be reconciled to your brother
and then come and offer your gift."
—MATTHEW 5:23–24

One of the most sobering experiences of my journey toward sexual wholeness was attempting to make a complete list of all those whom I had hurt as a result of my sexual sin. As I considered my own family, the families of my "partners," both of our future spouses, all future children, etc., etc., I was overwhelmed at how I had hurt a multitude of people that I knew and loved, people I never even knew, and people that hadn't even come into existence yet. I came face to face with the fact that my selfish pursuit of pleasure wound up causing far more damage than I could ever repair.

But oh, the desperate feeling of wanting to undo it all! I would have given anything to turn back the hands of time and make wiser decisions to protect myself and all the others that I affected, either knowingly or unknowingly. As willing as I was to go back to each and every person on my list to ask for forgiveness, my counselor warned, "Just because you are *willing* doesn't make it a *wise* thing to do." To express the point she was trying to make, she told me a story about an alcoholic named Bob....

Going Back to Our Old "Bartenders"

After a long, hard day, Bob is thinking he deserves a break. He goes into a bar because he thinks a good stiff drink would do the trick. The bartender behind the counter is always happy to see a paying customer! He is there to service Bob with a smile and pours him several drinks, one after the other. He even lends a listening ear to what a tough day Bob has had.

The bartender knows that drinking isn't good for Bob. He knows that too much alcohol will make Bob drunk, and that he will wake up in the morning regretting his indulgence, feeling even worse than when he left the office the day before. Yet, the bartender continues serving him drink after drink, fully cooperating in his customer's self-destruction.

After years of this pattern of insanity, Bob finally comes to his senses. He realizes that his drinking numbs his pain temporarily, but is causing his ultimate failure at work and at home. He comes to the conclusion that, in order to arrive at a new destination, he must travel a new path. He resolves that regardless of how hard his day goes, he will not have a drink.

Now I ask you, "Would it make any sense for Bob to go back to all of the bars he had visited to inform the various bartenders that he was not going to drink anymore?" Can't you imagine the bartenders thinking, "Yeah, right! So, why are you here?"

As ridiculous as this scenario sounds, this is exactly what your ex-boyfriends are probably thinking when we come back around to inform them that we are not going to be "that way" anymore. Okay, I know that stab may have hurt. But consider it an "incision" that needs to be made in order to remove the tumor that lies beneath the surface. As we venture into this next step, asking forgiveness, we have to be ever so careful to search our hearts on this issue before we run back into any bars. We must remember that even though *we* may have changed, those boyfriends who had no problem aiding us in our indulgences before may not have experienced the same transformation. They are still happy to see a girl come back around, assuming that what they want is more of the same thing.

As we consider all of those against whom we have trespassed, we may find ourselves anxious in a sense to seek reconciliation, because it means having a "valid" excuse for contacting our old flames once again. Do you understand that this is not remorse? Neither is it repentance. It is a trap that Satan is baiting just for you. He knows what kind of lure to use, because you have showed him where your weaknesses are. Don't give him that opportunity to ensnare you, sister. Don't even go there.

Are You Guilty, Ashamed, or Both?

Before we make a list of our trespasses and those we have trespassed against, it is important to understand the difference between guilt and shame. Daniel Green and Mel Lawrenz discuss the difference between these two states in *Why Do I Feel Like Hiding?: How to Overcome Shame and Guilt*. According to Green and Lawrenz, guilt and shame each have their own unique meanings:

> "Guilt" is the objective state of being responsible for a wrongdoing or transgression. Guilt is not an emotion or feeling (although we can feel guilty); rather, guilt is the status of being in the wrong. Its opposite is innocence. Guilt is independent of one's experience. For example, I may be guilty and not be aware of my guilt, or I may believe that I am guilty and actually be innocent.
>
> "Shame" is the subjective, personal, and painful emotional experience that occurs when one feels disconnected. It is a painful awareness of feeling inadequate, unworthy, and exposed.

When we feel shame, we often feel inhibited, or to some degree, like we want to hide..."[1]

Therefore, prior to making a list our trespasses, we must determine in each situation if we are truly guilty or merely feeling ashamed. Here is a case to illustrate:

As Libby made her list of persons she felt as if she had sinned against, she included her uncle. He began flirting with her when she was only twelve years old and he eventually attempted to molest her at age fifteen. Fortunately Libby prevented his success in his evil endeavor.

Her counselor asked, "Why do you feel the need to ask forgiveness of him? How do you feel that you wronged him?" Libby's response was, "My uncle divorced my aunt after that happened. I felt so bad. I must have done something to lead him on, and then I rejected him."

What Libby described is shame. She feels disconnected from her uncle because of the pain of the situation and the fact that he is no longer around. But is she guilty? No. His previous marriage problems had nothing to do with Libby. He was the offender in this case. Even if Libby's mannerisms at twelve to fifteen years of age caught her uncle's attention, he was the adult, and she was only a child. He had the responsibility of acting as an adult and protecting his niece, and he failed to do that. Her uncle is the one who is guilty. There is no need for Libby to ask forgiveness, only to recognize that she needs to forgive him.

Green and Lawrenz further explain that there are three forms of shame—moral shame, imposed shame, and natural shame. Moral shame is what we feel when we are in fact guilty. It prompts us toward confession. Imposed shame is a sense of shame imposed by someone else causing a disconnection. When the offender does not take responsibility for that disconnection, the common (but dysfunctional) response of the abuse victim is to take that shame on themselves. This is the type of shame Libby was experiencing in our case scenario.

The third type of shame is natural shame. It is a result of the disconnection between the human race and God because of our sin nature. This form of shame helps us recognize our failures and weaknesses, and leads us in brokenness back to God as the perfecter of our character. We can resolve this form of shame by receiving what Christ has done on the cross to remove our transgressions and our shame. Hebrews 12:2 says,

> *Let us fix our eyes on Jesus, the author and perfecter of our faith, who for the joy set before Him endured the cross, scorning its shame, and sat down at the right hand of the throne of God. Consider Him who endured such opposition from sinful men, so that you will not grow weary and lose heart.*

Making a List and Checking it Twice

Once you have determined the situations you were actually guilty in (not just ashamed, but truly guilty), then you are ready to make your list of those you have trespassed against. It would be helpful to state specifically the sin that you are guilty of (i.e., self-ishness, pride, manipulation, lust, ambition, revenge, idolatry, adultery, etc.). Once you have completed your list (and you may later realize that you have to add to it), put it down and ask yourself, "Am I *willing* to ask forgiveness from each of them?" If the answer is no, then spend as much time as you need praying that God will give you a humble spirit. The sinful things that led us into those relationships are often the same things that keep us from going back and asking forgiveness—things such as pride and self-ishness. It is hard to eat humble pie and admit that you were wrong, but it is a vital part of the healing process.

Once you feel willing to ask forgiveness from each of them, then *stop*! Okay, take a breather. You are willing, but is it *wise*? Is going back with a face-to-face apology what God is asking of you? Your next step is to pray long and hard about that question.

Willingness vs. Wisdom

Here are some challenging questions and thoughts to aid you in your decision:

1) WHOM HAVE I REALLY SINNED AGAINST?

Upon Nathan's reproach of David regarding his affair with Bathsheba (2 Samuel 11—covered in more detail in Chapter 10), David responds to Nathan in 2 Samuel 12:13, "I have sinned against the Lord." He did not say that he had sinned against Bathsheba, or even her husband, Uriah, whom he arranged to have killed. He said that he had sinned against God. Yes, we may bring injury upon one of God's creations, but it is against the Creator Himself that we ultimately commit the sin.

2) DO I BELIEVE I'M EXEMPT FROM FALLING AGAIN?

How many times have you made a proclamation of your intent not to have sex with an old boyfriend, only to find yourself back in the sack? One of the rules I try to live by is "Never say, 'I'll never do anything like that!'" As 1 Corinthians 10:12 says, "So, if you think you are standing firm, be careful that you don't fall!" Robin Norwood sums this principle up in her book, *Daily Meditations for Women Who Love Too Much*: "When people are really trying to change they don't talk about it much. They are too busy doing it."[2] If you feel the overwhelming need to go around telling all your old lovers that you are healed, you probably are not. If you are walking the walk, then you won't have to worry about talking the talk. Actions speak far louder than words.

3) AM I PREPARED TO BE AN EXAMPLE TO OTHERS?

When we make such proclamations to certain individuals, and then those individuals witness us struggle or even stumble and fall, doesn't that jeopardize our testimony? Simply by the fact that you've come back around, your old boyfriend is thinking, "Sure, you want me to think that you have changed, but you still want to be with me." How can others believe there is a God in heaven who gives us victory over this addiction if they sense you simply wanted to be in their presence once again, even if it was under the guise of confession?

4) AM I PREPARED TO BE CHALLENGED?

I believe such proclamations often serve subconsciously (or sadly enough, perhaps consciously!) as a challenge to men, to see if they can conquer your resolve. He may be thinking, "Yeah, you've changed! You are even better for me now!" Making yourself a target for his ego needs is not a wise move.

5) IS RECONNECTING WITH THIS PERSON PLACING EITHER OF US IN DANGER?

Wouldn't getting in touch with your old partners require yet another intimate exchange, whether by phone, in person, via e-mail, or whatever? Should you share your heart with someone who has already defiled it? Matthew 7:6 says, "Do not give to dogs what is sacred; do not throw your pearls to pigs. If you do, they may trample them under their feet, and then turn and tear you to pieces."

Asking Forgiveness

If, after prayerful consideration of all of these tidbits, you still feel the Holy Spirit guiding you to ask for forgiveness, I suggest the only safe way to do so is to write a brief, to-the-point note, requesting such. Don't wander into every detail God has been revealing to you regarding these issues. Don't update him on your whole life since you broke up. Simply make your apology. Have a trusted friend read the note to make sure you didn't include any "mixed messages" (i.e., "even though our relationship was great..." or "we had so much fun together, but...") Have them look for any "open doors" you may have left (i.e., "maybe when we see each other again someday" or "if the Lord ever leads us to start over you'd find I'm a different person...").

Also, don't include any photos or momentos! One girl told me that she was sending her old boyfriend a "We are really through this time, because I have changed" letter, and that she was going to send a cassette recording of some special songs along with it. I put the brakes on that idea when I reminded her that every time he listened to that tape, it would make him pine away for her! That wouldn't exactly communicate, "I want you to get over me and get on with your life," would it? Keep your confessions straight and to the point, and if you are serious about maintaining your sobriety, mail it without including a return address. You don't need to know his response. Whether he forgives you or not is his problem to deal with. And you don't need a direct apology from him in order to forgive him and move on with your life.

Examining the Exceptions

God would never ask you to do something that would injure someone else. To illustrate this point, let me use some brief examples. Would you ask for forgiveness from the wife of a man with whom you had an extramarital affair? What if she was unaware of the affair? If you were once in a relationship with a codependent man (one that came across as desperately insecure in the relationship), would it be fair to open up that can of worms again and reappear in his life now that he has finally moved on?

You get the idea. Don't look people up to vomit in their lap just because you feel the need to vomit. It may make *you* feel better, but ask yourself, "How will it make *them* feel?" If you have to vomit up a confession, then do it in a safe place, such as with a counselor or trusted girlfriend.

Consider this question—would God expect you to do something that would completely endanger all that you have accomplished in your journey toward wholeness? Don't make the mistake that I did, and think, "He made me so weak in the knees before, but I want to see how strong I can be around him now!" Thank God, my counselor had the courage to ask me, "Why on earth would you want to go back to the junkie who once supplied your drug? Don't you understand that *he* is your addiction?" As a fellow Woman at the Well put it recently, "Don't jump into a lion's den and stick your head in a lion's mouth, and then pray that God will save you from the lions!"

You Are Not His Savior

I have shared this information about asking forgiveness with many women, and occasionally the response I get from some Christian women is, "I'm going to go ahead and get in touch with him anyway. It's not because I want to rekindle the relationship. It is because he needs the Lord! I'm going to witness to him and save him from ruining his life." These women think they are being so "selfless" to want to do this, but I dare to challenge that assumption. If they were to really examine their hearts over that decision, they would often find "selfishness" at the root of it. In his book, *Biblical Basis of Christian Counseling for People Helpers*, Gary Collins gives us insight into this motive:

> Have you ever heard of the "messiah complex"?
>
> This isn't a psychiatric diagnosis or a condition that gets listed in books on abnormal psychology. Instead, the messiah complex refers to the tendency for caring people, counselors included, to become rescuers who try to deliver others from their problems and difficult life circumstances. At times, almost all of

us want to be like messiahs, saving people from their dysfunctional families, enslaving addictions, or self-destructive lifestyles.

I have a friend who has spent all of his adult life working in a private practice and teaching counseling skills to graduate students. His years of experience have shown that when counselors try to be rescuers, the rescuers almost always end up being hurt. Even so, my friend still is tempted at times to be like a messiah. "It would be nice if I could rescue people from their pain and release them from their problems," he has told his students. "But whenever I am tempted to try taking on that role, I remember how powerless I am and I think about what happened to the real Messiah. He was crucified."[3]

Realize that your old boyfriend doesn't need you, he needs the Lord. And the Lord is big enough to send laborers into his life. As harsh as it sounds, you may not be the best laborer to witness to him anyway. Your testimony has already been jeopardized, because of your past romantic interest in him. If you want to have a part in his salvation, then pray that God will send someone to whom your old flame will show respect and listen. Pray for his highest good. Pray that he has a major revelation from God. And if you want to be a witness, remember that actions speak louder than words. *Show him* that Christ has changed your life, by living differently than you did before. Running back for his attention (even if it is to witness to him) is something you would have done in your past. This time, trust in the Lord to bring salvation. You can't save anyone. The Lord desires his salvation more than you do, and He will be faithful to send laborers into his life whose testimony will not be jeopardized by their previous romantic interest in him.

Breaking Soul Ties

This process of asking forgiveness of our trespasses is not about reclaiming just your body. This is about reclaiming your soul.

Your old lover no longer has your body, but do soul ties still remain between the two of you? Is there still a possibility in your mind that he could be the one you will marry? Do you still obsess about him on occasion? Do you still look for opportunities to cross his path?

Imagine two construction-paper hearts, one black and one red. Glue is applied between them, and they bond for a little while. Then, when those two hearts are separated, what happens? Wherever the bonding agent has been (the glue), there will be shreds of black fibers on the red heart and fibers of the red heart stuck to the black. Then when those two hearts go and bond again with other colored hearts, they accumulate even more excess fibers and lose many of their own as well. Even though two hearts are separated, there is still a part of the other person that you carry around long after the separation. It is a part of their soul. And he carries around a part of yours. Even if you never had sex with him, if you gave him your heart, you lost a part of your soul in the process. This intimate connection is called a "soul tie."

Proverbs 4:23 tells us, "Above all else, guard your heart, for it is the wellspring of life." If you have not guarded your heart as you should have in the past, and a part of your soul is still attached to someone out there, take refuge in Psalm 23:3—"He restores my soul..." What do you have to do in order to reclaim your heart and allow God to restore your soul? Deuteronomy 6:5 says, "Love the Lord your God with all your heart *and with all your soul* and with all your strength." In other words, love God like you've never loved any man before, and that love relationship in itself will break soul ties and heal many wounds. Matthew 11:28–29 says, "Come to Me, all you who are weary and burdened, and I will give you rest. Take My yoke upon you and learn from Me, for I am gentle and humble in heart, and you will find rest for your souls." Doesn't "rest for our souls" sound so inviting after the torment of so many soul ties in the past? Envision hiding underneath the shadow of

God's wing, resting peacefully in Him, and there you will discover the restoration your soul longs for.

Tonight when you go to bed, rather than entertain obsessive thoughts about some guy, imagine yourself with your new Love. Forget the lame compliments you have hoped for from admirers in the past and remember the compliment Christ gave you when His love for you held Him on the cross. Rather than longing for a man to open doors for you, meditate on the door of eternal salvation Christ has opened for you. No greater gift could anyone give to you than that which God gift-wrapped on Christmas Eve and Easter morning! Face it, girl, God is enamored with you, and He cares enough to send the *very best!*

QUESTIONS FOR INTROSPECTION:

• Who are the individuals (known or unknown) against whom you are guilty of trespassing due to your sexual sin or emotional entanglements? (Make a separate list if necessary.)

• Are there any persons in your past who have attempted to impose shame on you because of their failure to recognize their own guilt or to accept responsibility for their actions?

- Are there any "bartenders" (previous partners) you are tempted to visit in order to tell them you have "stopped drinking"?

- Do you look for "valid" excuses to revisit your old partners?

- Are you willing to pursue sexual purity and guard your heart even if it means avoiding contact with old partners?

- Do you have a "messiah complex"? Do you feel that the Lord can't accomplish His divine will without *your* personal involvement?

- Do you trust God enough to send laborers into your old partners' lives to bring them to salvation? Are you willing to let go of that relationship and let God have His way in that person's life, even if it does not include you?

• Are there soul ties that you need to ask the Lord to break? Are you willing to surrender all connections to those individuals for the sake of your relationship with Christ and with your current or future husband?

• What do you stand to gain from such surrender? How do you envision your life changing, once you are set free from soul ties and from your guilt of sins committed against others?

CHAPTER NINE

Forgiving Those Who Trespass

"For if you forgive men when they sin against you,
your heavenly Father will also forgive you.
But if you do not forgive men their sins, your Father
will not forgive your sins."
—MATTHEW 6:14

Every time someone mentioned the word "Daddy," Leann's stomach churned. Each time she saw a father and young daughter playing or holding hands, she hung her head. Whenever her pastor would preach about "God the Father," Leann wanted to sneak out of the back of the sanctuary.

Her anger continued to rage over the daddy she never had. Oh, she had a father alright, but he had never been a daddy to her. In the early years, he was never around. He worked all day, then came home, ate dinner, and escaped to his workshop out back. As a young girl, Leann anxiously anticipated her dad walking through the door, covered in grease with lunchbox in hand. But after years of getting not much more than a pat on the head as he walked right by her on his way to the dinner table, Leann learned that she shouldn't get her hopes up too high.

As the years passed on, Leann learned she could get her

father's undivided attention when she exasperated her mother to the point of utter frustration. When Mom reached her limit with Leann, she would shout out the back door toward the workshop, "You need to come and deal with your daughter!" Ah, finally he would pay attention to her the only way he knew how—with his belt.

As an adult woman, Leann's anger continued to boil inside of her, spewing out at her own husband and children. "I always swore I'd never treat my family like my dad treated us, but I get so angry!" she sobbed to God one day in prayer. The Holy Spirit spoke to her and told her that until she tried to understand why her dad was the kind of father he was, she would never be the kind of mother she wanted to be. Leann continued praying for several weeks, and finally found the courage to write her dad a letter:

> I never really knew you, Dad. I wanted to desperately, but as a child, I never knew the questions to ask. Now that I am an adult, I still have so many questions. I wish we could find an opportunity to spend some time together. I want to hear about your childhood. I want to know the events that shaped your life. I want to be able to pass on our family history to my children, but I don't even know what that history consists of. I want to know you. Can we please make some time to talk?

Several weeks later, her father responded with an invitation for a family camping trip. Would this be the opportunity she was hoping for? She didn't want to get her hopes up only to have them dashed once again, but she was willing to take that chance.

On the second day of the trip, Leann was at a camp playground with her husband and children. Her dad approached, grabbed her by the hand, and began walking toward a dock on the lake. Startled by his forwardness, Leann couldn't help feeling awkward holding his hand. It was such an unfamiliar sensation. But oh, how she had longed for it all her life. She finally resolved that she was not going to reject him after so many years of missing this very thing.

As they walked, Dad began telling stories from as far back as he could remember. These stories brought tears to both their eyes—stories about his father's post-war trauma, mental illness, and suicide attempts. Stories of his mother's multiple lovers, divorces, and inability to care for him. Stories of his stepmother's abuse. Stories of his stepfather's anger and neglect. He was tossed back and forth from mother to father to grandparents and uncles, because no one wanted him.

"Why have you never told me these things, Daddy?" Leann asked, realizing that it was the first time since she was a young girl that she had called him "Daddy."

"I never knew how. I guess I thought if I never talked about it, it would all go away. Leann, I realize that I was never the father that you deserved, but I tried desperately to give you a better life than what I had. I failed at a lot of things, but I succeeded at what I thought was most important.

"I refused to become an alcoholic like my father. I tried my best to control my temper. I refused to bail out of my marriage at the times when the going got tough. I made sure you always had a house to come home to and food on the table. And I was determined to keep our family together, regardless of how hard it was."

Funny how looking at her childhood through her father's eyes that weekend completely changed Leann's perspective. She felt ashamed that she had always seen the bad side of her father, never recognizing how he had been such a good provider and had held their family together through thick and thin. Her eyes had always been focused on herself and upon what she had missed out on. She had never given much thought to the wounds her father still carried around from his own childhood, crippling him emotionally.

Hurting People Hurt People

One of the most valuable lessons one can learn in this lifetime is that *hurting people hurt people*. Sure, it is easy to throw a stone at the child abuser, the alcoholic, or the disconnected husband or father. If we look beyond their weakness to their needs, however, what will we find? Chances are we will find feelings of inadequacy, hostilities raging, and depression clouding most every thought. We will find someone who has been traumatized beyond imagination, and who has few coping mechanisms other than to lash out at innocent people. In *Handbook to Happiness: A Guide to Victorious Living and Effective Counseling*, Charles R. Solomon states,

> ...hostility is sometimes projected onto someone else (displaced hostility), usually a person who does not deserve it. The pressure is relieved to some extent by acting out hostility, but additional guilt is incurred, which serves to increase the frustration, and another hostile act is committed. On and on the cycle goes.[1]

Focus on the Family once aired a speech on their radio show given by author and speaker Frank Peretti. Just one year after the tragic Columbine High School massacre in Littleton, Colorado, Frank masterfully drew our attention behind the eyes of the gunmen. He shared personal diary entries that gave a glimpse into the pain these young men experienced as they were mocked, insulted, humiliated, tormented, and rejected by their peers. The note written by the gunmen before the shooting was indicative of the hostility boiling inside them. "And now you will all pay for how you have treated me!" one of the teenage boys wrote. His pain and hostility ran so deep that he ended his own life in the midst of the rampage shooting as well.

As hard as it is to look beyond the gunmen's weaknesses to their needs, we must understand that it is hurting people who hurt people. The reason this concept is so important is because chances are, as a Woman at the Well, you are a hurting person. And as long as you are carrying around that hurt and hostility toward your trespassers, you are a danger to yourself and to others. And sadly, you usually hurt the ones you love the most.

Hostility Eats Us Alive

Not only does your frustration and hostility over how others have harmed or neglected you affect your relationships with your loved ones, it also has a devastating affect on your own mind, emotions, soul, and even your health. Let's continue with more of Charles Solomon's insights on hostility and depression from *Handbook to Happiness: A Guide to Victorious Living & Effective Counseling:*

> ...frustration can affect the emotions, another area of the soul... A common effect on the emotions is depression. Hostility kept inward becomes depression. We push against ourselves. We take it out on ourselves instead of taking it out on someone else. We beat ourselves severely about the head and shoulders, which causes to us to be depressed, anxious, and tied up in knots. A more homespun definition of depression is that of an internal temper tantrum. This can be simple depression or it can become more severe and be termed reactive depression or clinical depression. Still these are not, at their root, mental problems or real emotional problems. They are symptoms of a deeper problem. The problem is usually treated by attempting to rid the afflicted one of the anxiety and depression that has been bottled up inside.
>
> This anxiety and depression is usually contained until it is no longer possible to restrict it to the domain of the soul. Then it manifests itself in the body as a psychosomatic or psychophysiological symptom... Ultimately, these physical or psychosomatic

symptoms are spiritual problems; since the only complete answer is spiritual, the problem must be spiritual as well.[2]

To what spiritual problem is Solomon referring? The unforgiveness that we consciously or subconsciously harbor within our hearts toward those who have wronged us. What complete answer is Solomon suggesting? Forgiving those who trespass against us.

Christ's Example

Before we can begin to grasp how to forgive those who have trespassed against us, we must remember the example that Christ gave us. There are beautiful illustrations of Christ's forgiveness in contemporary stories and scriptural parables. Let's look at a couple of those.

In Luke 15:11–32, we read how the prodigal son insisted on his share of his father's inheritance, only to go out into the world and squander it. He later chose to return home to beg his father's forgiveness and to serve as a slave in his father's household to make restitution. Rather than sending his son away, reciting a lecture on responsible living, or even retorting with an "I told you so," the father ran to embrace his son, gave him a ring and a robe, and killed a fattened calf to celebrate his son's return.

Let's rewrite this Scripture to parallel our stories... We took the heart, soul, and body that God gave us, ran into the arms of men, and squandered them away on what we thought would bring fulfillment, only to find that stagnant water didn't satisfy us. In brokenness and desperation, we return to God as a last resort. But rather than reject us as our actions deserve, God looks beyond our weakness to our needs and runs anxiously to meet us. He wraps a robe of righteousness around His beloved, slides a wedding ring on her finger, and prepares a spiritual feast before us. His heart leaps for joy that his daughter has returned home where she belongs. His forgiveness is complete and He celebrates our restoration.

Or imagine standing in a courtroom before a judge. You have been accused of living an ungodly life and the suggested punishment is death. The prosecuting attorney asks the judge's permission to show a film to the jury. The judge concedes, the lights dim, and the footage begins to roll. To your shock and dismay, you realize that the prosecuting attorney is Satan himself and he has it all on video—every temptation you've succumbed to, every vengeful thought you've ever had, every selfish deed you'd ever done, every act of immorality right there on film. You panic. There is no defense for you. The proof of your ungodly life is too evident. The film finally ends, the lights come on, and your defense attorney is given a chance to speak. Rather than say a word, He merely removes his shirt to reveal multiple bloody stripes on His back. "Your Honor," He states, "This woman's punishment has already been carried out. She has been pardoned." Case closed. That is forgiveness. You walk out of the courtroom a free woman.

Being Imitators of Christ

Now let's apply these examples to our own dilemmas. Others have hurt us. They've rejected us. They've wounded us. They've robbed us of our dignity, our hope, and our wholeness. There is no excuse for what they have done to us. But when we remember how Christ has forgiven us of even our most heinous trespasses against Him, we have no excuse not to be imitators of Christ. In Matthew 6:12, Jesus is teaching His followers to pray and includes the phrase, "Forgive us our trespasses, as we forgive those who trespass against us." This is the only part of the Lord's Prayer that is followed by a commentary. "For if you forgive men when they sin against you, your heavenly Father will also forgive you. But if you do not forgive men their sins, your Father will not forgive your sins" (Matthew 6:14–15). Therefore, we would do well to remember that forgiveness is a two-way street. If we expect to receive God's forgiveness, we must exercise forgiveness of others, regardless of how deeply that sin hurt us.

How many times should we forgive someone? In Matthew 18:21–22, we see Peter ask Jesus, "Lord, how many times shall I forgive my brother when he sins against me? Up to seven times?" Jesus' response is, "I tell you, not seven times, but seventy-seven times."

Ideally, someday your forgiveness of your offenders will lead them to a greater understanding of God's mercy. Eventually, trust may even be restored in the relationship, just as Jesus trusted Peter after He forgave him for his three denials.

But what if the person isn't remorseful of their offense? Do you need to forgive then? Again, let's follow Christ's example. Even as He was dying on the cross at the hands of an angry mob, some of His last words were, "Father, forgive them, for they do not know what they are doing" (Luke 23:34). The crowd showed no remorse for their barbaric behavior, yet Christ again reached beyond their weakness to their needs. People needed forgiveness then, and people need forgiveness now.

President Richard Nixon once said, "When you hate others and refuse to forgive, you are the one who really loses in the end. When there is forgiveness between people, the forgiver and the offender both benefit."

A Bitter Land vs. A Better Land

One of the decisions you must make when someone offends you is, "*Will I choose to live in a bitter land or in a better land?*" In other words, are you going to allow their transgressions to move you to a less desirable place in your life where bitterness, resentment, and hostility eat away at your heart and soul? Or are you going to look for how you have personally grown through such an experience and allow the situation to move you to a place of greater understanding, compassion, and maturity?

As we practice being imitators of Christ, we are transformed into His likeness and thus are able to overcome trials and help others do the same. And if you ask yourself, "Where would I be had this not happened to me?" the truth is that you probably wouldn't be depending as fully on God as you are right now. You'd probably be living life out of your own strength and not looking to God for His strength.

I frequently recite the following words to keep me from becoming bitter or discouraged about my past: *My journey toward recovery has also been my pathway toward God.* Over the past several years of struggling to overcome love addiction, I've had to pursue God like I never would have otherwise. For the discovery that I have made in Jesus Christ, I am truly grateful. As Paul wrote in Romans 5:3–4, I will rejoice in my sufferings because I know that suffering produces perseverance; perseverance, character; and character, hope.

Another benefit to choosing a better land instead of a bitter land is that the anger and abuse that has occurred in your family generation after generation can finally come to an end. Sure, it's easy to focus on what your parents did or didn't do right, but chances are they were repeating the same mistakes their parents and their grandparents made. These dysfunctional cycles are called *generational curses*, and guess what? YOU, if you are not already, will be the next generation of parents in your family! The rope that has bound your family together is being passed to you, and you must decide if you are going to make a hangman's noose or a pretty bow out of it. You must decide if you are going to continue this vicious cycle by passing these behaviors down to your own children, or if you are going to draw the line in the sand and say, "The buck stops with me, Satan! You will not have a hold on this family any longer because I am God's chosen instrument to bring healing to my family's past, joy to its present, and hope to its future!"

Forgiving Yourself

As we make a list of all those individuals who have brought us harm, don't we have to include ourselves? Haven't we perhaps brought ourselves the most harm? While forgiving our offenders can certainly be a struggle, forgiving ourselves poses perhaps one of the greatest challenges of all!

I recall the many times that I confided in a friend, "I have forgiven every single person I can possibly recall, but I can't forgive myself." I felt that I should have known better than to do the things I was guilty of. Being raised in the church added to my guilt and shame. I flat-out rebelled against everything I knew to be right. I rebelled against God, against my parents, against my future husband, and against my own conscience. But a friend reminded me that once I had repented from my sin, to continue holding on to any guilt was to say, in essence, that what Christ did on the cross *wasn't enough* for me. With that thought came conviction that it was my lack of faith in what Christ did on the cross that kept my grip firm on my own sense of unforgiveness. Once I came to firmly believe Christ's words in John 19:30 when He said, "It is finished," I could be finished with self-condemnation.

Another effective exercise a counselor walked me through was to place an empty chair in front of a chair that I occupied and pretend that "Shannon at age fifteen" (the age I became sexually active) was sitting across from me. She instructed me to tell the fifteen-year-old Shannon anything and everything I felt that I needed to. The thought of pouring out your heart to an empty chair may seem strange to you, but if you continue to struggle with not being able to forgive yourself because of your own transgressions, I highly recommend this exercise.

As I removed my focus from my current self to the confused teenager I once was, I felt my heart leap out of my chest toward this imaginary counterpart. I knew that at age fifteen, Shannon was desperately hurting and was in need of attention, instruction, and guidance—not judgment. I felt as if I needed to warn her about the detours that she was about to take off of God's path and how they would lead to further isolation and resentment. Rather than condemnation, I felt complete sympathy and compassion for her. So why hadn't I felt that way about my thirty-year old self? After that point, I did. I began to see that I, too, was a person in need of mercy and grace.

My countenance was completely changed after that revelation. Prior to that experience, I don't ever recall looking into a mirror when I didn't dislike the reflection I saw. I had harsh lines on my forehead and on the bridge of my nose from the scowl I typically wore on my face. But over the past few years, I have caught glimpses of myself in the mirror and actually been at peace with my own reflection. I believe it is God's peace, which passes all under-standing, that has brought such a change—not only in my heart and soul, but in my face as well.

Reaching the point of having a healthy love of ourselves (not vanity, but love) is so important, because Leviticus 19:18 tells us to love our neighbors *as* ourselves. But how can you love your neighbor if you *don't* love yourself? You can't give something you don't have, and you are only able to love others to the extent that you love yourself. I encourage you to forgive yourself, so that you can forgive others. Then you can love yourself more fully, and love others more completely.

Last But Not Least—Forgiving God

We all know in our minds that God is incapable of sin, yet in our hearts, many of us are angry at God, whether we've ever allowed ourselves to admit it or not. It may not be true in every case, but the intense emotional needs of many Women at the Well stem from the lack of emotional nurturing they experienced from their fathers. To make matters worse, as we attended church, we learned about God being our "Father." It was easy to feel repulsed by God if He was anything like what we envisioned our earthly fathers to be.

I once witnessed a group counseling member snap at the leader, "Don't tell me about God the Father loving me, when my own father raped me again and again!" The point was well taken. The counselor then referred to God as a "Mother," "Lover," or "Friend" from that session on. I thought this was a clever move on her part, in light of the fact that the message was still clear: we serve a loving, nurturing God who cares deeply for us and would never hurt us.

If the word "Father" brings up bitterness in your mind as well, then use one of the many other references to God (the Bible is full of them—Comforter, Redeemer, Refuge, etc.). As you make peace with your earthly father, you may also discover a much greater peace with your Heavenly Father.

In his book entitled *Father Hunger*, Robert McGee explains the phenomenon of how women who never felt the genuine love of a father as a child often continue searching for a father figure in their romantic pursuits as an adult.

> Many women hunger so for a father's love that they easily fall for men who seem to be everything they had hoped for as little girls needing a daddy. Perhaps a male supervisor with whom a woman spends long hours at work may seem to be an irresistible magnet. Others become infatuated with the pastor at church who seems so loving and kind. Often these women are married with children of their own, but the attraction can be very insidious and powerful.[3]

McGee expounds on this point further by exploring the heart of a woman who developed this sort of obsession toward her boss and ended up blaming God for not providing the love she needed as a small child.

If you are feeling angry at God because of the absence of a loving father in your childhood, that is okay. God knows your heart, so you don't have to pretend to hide your feelings from Him. You are right. It wasn't fair for you to grow up with such an abusive father, or an alcoholic father, or an absentee father. You shouldn't be suffering the intense pain you may feel right now—it's not your fault. But know that it isn't God's fault, either. I agree with Robert McGee as he concludes this saga by saying,

> ...I truly believe God understands those intensely negative feelings we have toward Him. He will patiently wait as we go to Him crying, kicking, and screaming. And He will be there with His arms held out to us when we finish venting our feelings.
>
> ...The sooner you are willing to become brutally honest, the sooner you can work through the pain that has been holding you captive for so long.
>
> One reason we need to be honest about our feelings is that we may be wrong. Feelings can easily fool us. But if we're not honest about them, we never get around to discovering the truth. I encourage you to be completely honest about any feelings you have toward God, especially those you may not even want to admit to yourself. God honors truth. He will not be judgmental if you express how you honestly feel. Spend some time trying to identify any negative feelings you may have of God as a father.[4]

There is one final note about relating to God that I would like to make. Youth minister, author, and speaker Josh McDowell coined the phrase, "Rules without relationships lead to rebellion." When I heard him make this powerful statement, at the American Association of Christian Counselors' World Conference in 1997, the truth of it cut right through to my heart. Didn't many of us rebel from our parent's rules because of the lack of a healthy relationship with them? Well, the same thing is true with God. It is so easy for us to rebel if we try to live by His rules, but fail to pursue a real relationship with Him. The fact that many of us have known about the Ten Commandments, but so few of us have lived by them, is proof that until we have an intimate love relationship with God, the rules are impossible to follow.

If you desire to make better choices, then invest in a better relationship with Christ. If you want to improve the quality of your life, start by improving the quality of your relationship with God.

I am the vine; you are the branches. If a [woman] *remains in Me and I in* [her], [she] *will bear much fruit; apart from Me you can do nothing... If you remain in Me and My words remain in you, ask whatever you wish, and it will be given you"* (John 15:5,7).

QUESTIONS FOR INTROSPECTION:

• If your father or mother is someone who has caused you harm, what hurts can you identify in their lives that may have driven them to inflict such pain?

• How has hostility toward others affected your emotional, mental, spiritual, and/or physical health?

• Who are some of the other people in your life that have caused you harm?

• Is forgiving them difficult for you? Why or why not?

• Is there anything holding you back from imitating Christ's forgiveness? If so, how can that roadblock be dealt with?

• Would *not* forgiving them result in even more difficulty? How so?

• As a result of the pain that has been inflicted upon you by others, how can you choose a better land instead of a bitter land?

- Are there things for which you have not forgiven yourself? Do you believe that what Christ did for you on the cross was enough to set you free, or do you think that your sin is so great that you need a "special" miracle to set you free?

- Are there things that cause you to blame God? Have you confessed your anger toward Him?

- How, specifically, can you improve the quality of your relationship with God so that living by His rules will bring safety and joy, not rebellion?

CHAPTER TEN

Better Boundaries

"Watch and pray that you may not enter into temptation;
the spirit is indeed willing but the flesh is weak."
—MARK 14:38

Jenny was eight years old when her parents bought a wooded lot and began building a home in a new development near the Everglades in Florida. Each week her family would drive out to the location and her parents would tell her to go play while they carefully inspected the craftsmanship of each detail of the new house.

At the end of their new street was a low-lying valley full of undeveloped lots. Spring rains had been heavy and had transformed this land into a fascinating quagmire full of algae, tadpoles, etc. One day, while splashing around in this newfound playground, Jenny was amazed to discover a little lizard—no, it was a tiny baby alligator! She held it in the palm of her hand and stroked its scaly backside. She affectionately named him Alley Gator, took an oath to keep their friendship a secret, and anxiously anticipated getting moved in so that they could have more playtimes together.

The building project lingered on throughout the hot summer and when September came, Jenny's family finally moved into their dream home. The first day of school soon came around, and Jenny looked forward to making new friends. After school, Jenny and the neighboring kids hopped off the school bus in front of the development. "Would you like to meet my other friend?" Jenny asked.

"Sure!" replied the curious students, and they followed her to the end of the street to the swampy valley. "What's your friend's name?"

"Alley." Then Jenny slammed her books to the ground, removed her shoes and socks, rolled up her pant legs, and began wading through the water beckoning, "Here, Alley! I have some friends who want to meet you!"

In a flash Jenny began sinking quickly down into the mud, screaming with terror. Before the other children even knew what was happening, Jenny had disappeared beneath the surface. Only bubbles remained.

By the time the police and animal control arrived, there was no hope of retrieving Jenny's body alive. They explained that, rather than moving to deeper waters, alligators will adapt to their surroundings by burrowing deep into the mud, and that they trap their prey by capturing it in their jaws and dragging it down into their burrow to suffocate.

As difficult as this story is to imagine, this is a perfect analogy for how quickly innocent victims get snatched up and devoured by "baby pet alligator" sins. As humans, we often lack the judgement necessary to discern when Satan is disguising himself and tempting us with something that looks oh, so innocent. Without clearly established boundaries, there is no guarantee Satan's jaws will not catch us off guard and drag us under for the battle of our lives.

The Safe Sex Myth

In examining boundaries, let's first talk about ensuring optimum physical health by dispelling the "safe sex" myth. The only safe sex is no sex, or married sex between two partners who have had no prior sexual involvement. Aside from that, there is no

100 percent guarantee. There have been tons of books written on this topic as well, so again, we can't begin to do it justice. But let's step back and look at the big picture for a moment.

Let's define "monogamy." You'd be surprised how many young people think monogamy is having sex with only one partner… at a time! That is actually "serial monogamy," where you are only in one bed at a time—perhaps for long periods of time—but you are bed-hopping just the same. True monogamy is having sex with only one partner for a lifetime. What is the only way you can be 100 percent certain that your sexual partner is also your lifetime partner? To have a lifelong marriage commitment in place first. You must be married (not in love, going steady, or even engaged) to guarantee this is truly the one God ordained for you to have sex with. Ask an older married woman how many times she thought she was in love, going steady, or was even proposed to by a gentleman prior to ever marrying her husband. If we had sex with every guy we thought was a possible future husband, we'd endanger ourselves a great deal.

Speaking of that danger, according to the Medical Institute for Sexual Health (MISH), there are twenty to twenty-five significant types of sexually transmitted diseases (STDs). The Center for Disease Control (CDC) reported in 1992 the following statistics: There are twelve million newly infected people each year. One in four Americans between fifteen and fifty-five years of age is now infected with a viral STD (one that cannot be treated with antibiotics). Sixty-three percent of all STD infection occurs in persons less than twenty-five years of age. MISH also reports that one in every four people newly infected with HIV is younger than twenty-two years of age.

If you weren't hearing so much about HIV, you'd hear a lot more about HPV (Human Papillomavirus) and how it infects up to forty-six percent of some groups of sexually active singles. The list of diseases and their devastating effects on women today is startling. They result in things such as genital warts, cervical cancer, and even sterility. If you ever hope to have your own children someday or even live to see your golden years, I pray that you will not allow Satan to deceive you into believing you can have sex without any physical consequences. With every new partner comes a life-or-death roll of the dice. And don't fool yourself into thinking that condoms are the answer. According to MISH, they often fail to provide proper protection against pregnancy, the transmission of HIV, and many other diseases. Besides, a condom can only protect the portion of the body it covers. There is no condom for your heart or your soul.

Beyond the Physical

Which leads us to our next topic—your emotional and mental health. MISH reports that adolescent girls are four times more likely to commit suicide after their first sexual encounter. What does that tell you? That with the sexual bond comes an emotional bond, and when that bond is broken, it has a devastating effect on our mind and emotions. In addition to depression, there are many other aspects of "romantic pursuits" that pose internal threats such as stress, anxiety, low self-esteem, guilt, shame, and the list goes on and on.

How can you possibly guard your heart if you continue tossing it around to any man who will catch it and caress it for a while? How can we keep our minds focused on eternal things and set our agendas according to God's plan each day if we are willing to rearrange our schedule at a man's beckoning call? We have to set emotional boundaries as well as physical boundaries in order to keep our hearts intact and our minds steadfast.

Last but not least, your spiritual health is something that is far too precious to jeopardize. Imagine how you would feel standing at the altar if your groom whispered in your ear, "Honey, I love you so much that I am willing to give up nine of my ten other girlfriends!" Forget the nine he's agreed to give up, you want to know about the one that he plans to hold onto, right? Doesn't God have the right to feel that way when we lovingly surrender our family life, our school life, our work life, yet hold back our love life, or our thought life, or even a small piece of our heart reserved for that special someone?

God is a jealous God (Exodus 20:5), and He is the giver of all good gifts. If your special someone isn't a gift from the Lord, but one that you have pursued and captured by your own schemes, then it is a matter of time before you discover that he's not a very good gift after all. In fully surrendering even your love life, you are saying to God, "*Lord, I trust You. I am willing to be patient until You are ready to give me the gifts that You have for me.*"

One of the gifts that He has for you right now is one of complete intimacy with Him alone. Once you get spoiled to letting God love you full time, you'll be a lot more leery of other men. But your affair with the Lord is one that you never have to give up! You can take this affair right into your marriage and your husband won't even mind. Hopefully, he'll be having a similar affair. A love relationship with Jesus is one that will sustain you through singleness and marriage, through sickness and health, through poverty and wealth. There is no other way to achieve optimum spiritual health than through this sustaining love relationship with the Lord.

Before we examine secure boundaries, let's talk about some slippery boundaries—those that people often mistake as being safe, but that actually set them up to be snatched and dragged down into the mud...

Slippery Cyberspace

While sitting in front of a computer in the privacy of your own home may provide a feeling of safety and security, the Internet has made it possible for Satan to drag temptation right into your house on a silver platter. In an article entitled "Webstruck," published by *Aspire* magazine, Beth J. Lueders explores how even Christian women are enticed into unhealthy relationships on the Internet.

Dorothy opened the colored-button world of America Online, where, thanks to modern technology, she could enter a room full of people to meet with places to go. Amazed by all the dazzling options before her, she had double clicked her mouse on People Connection, which zipped her to the next stops on the World Wide Web of Romance: The Meeting Place and finally Chance Encounters.

The 57-year-old homemaker, much like her ancestor, Eve, was enthralled by the lush garden before her and the come-hither talk that promised to open her eyes. A nibble on the forbidden fruit of a chance encounter with an attentive man tasted refreshingly sweet. Surely a few minutes of chatting with a stranger across the country couldn't hurt, Dorothy reasoned.

But what started two years ago as a way to write to friends eventually turned into a twisted addiction for an upper-middle class Christian woman.[1]

The article continues on to say how Dorothy now neglects her family, prayer groups and Bible studies, spending eight hours per day on the Internet. She even flew to California to meet a chat-room friend struggling through his divorce. Her children were sure they were having an affair. I've seen it happen in my own circle of friends. One (married eight years with two children) confided that she flew across the country under the pretense of reuniting with old high-school buddies, only to meet an Internet friend for a weekend at a hotel. Having recognized the magnitude of her sin and how addictive such cyberspace relationships are, she continues to struggle to maintain emotional control every time she sits down at her computer.

Quenching the Flame or Fueling It?

Another "seemingly harmless" sin was discussed in an earlier chapter, but I think that the topic of masturbation is worth revisiting here. I'm often told by single women struggling to maintain sexual purity that their "preventative measures" against premarital sex include masturbating prior to going out on a date, so they won't make a decision about sexual activity based on current physical needs. This makes about as much sense as drinking a bottle of wine before you go out to a bar so that you won't be tempted to drink as much!

The fact that some women have subscribed to this philosophy saddens me for several reasons. First, why would anyone in her right mind go out with a man knowing that he is going to exert sexual pressure? Shouldn't she know his character well enough prior to going out with him to trust that there would be no sexual expectations? Second, since when is having an orgasm a physical need? Self-control is what we need! We won't explode if we don't have an orgasm. We are not animals who operate merely by instinct. We are human beings created in the image of God.

Many people live a celibate life without masturbation. Many refuse to masturbate as an outlet for their sexual desires because they have figured out that masturbating doesn't quench any flame, but rather fuels the fire of sexual desire. One Woman at the Well recently confirmed my belief when she bluntly stated that she can't masturbate before a date and then expect to remain in control. She said, "All I can think about that night is how disappointed I was with the masturbation experience and how it would be more satisfying to give in and have sex." There's honesty for you. Masturbation doesn't quench any flames. It only fuels them.

Pulling In the Reins

Leading seminars on saving sex until marriage, I am amazed and disappointed at the number of young people who insist that they have healthy boundaries as long as they do not allow vaginal intercourse (or "go all the way!"). Aside from that, anything else is fair game to many, including oral or anal sex. Young people are startled to hear how other forms of sex are as dangerous when it comes to transmitting diseases. So, they re-establish their boundaries to exclude such sexual activity, but maintain that fondling of the genitals is still acceptable. Then I ask them, "Do you think you and your partner can arouse each other to that point and then maintain your commitment to abstaining from sexual intercourse until you are married?" I expound by reminding them that, at age sixteen to eighteen, they have anywhere from five to ten years or more before marriage. That is like throwing gas on a campfire, but expecting the forest not to burn down for another ten years.

The young audiences usually agree to amend their boundaries, but still say that breast stimulation is "safe." I respond with how arousing that activity is for a woman, the sexual chemicals that are released in her brain with such stimulation, and the sacredness of her breasts as being so close to her heart and also where her babies will someday nurse for their survival.

"Okay! Fine! We'll just make out then!" they say in frustration. So, we talk about how French kissing is designed to "get your juices flowing," and as such, is actually foreplay to sexual activity (that is why you don't French kiss your parents). To use someone to satisfy your own selfish desires to passionately kiss or be kissed isn't respectful. "After all," I remind them, "that person you engage in passionate kissing with is more than likely going to be someone *else's* spouse someday. How would you feel about someone French kissing *your* future spouse and getting them all aroused before you ever marry them?"

Believe it or not, before the weekend seminar is over, the vast majority of young people make commitments not only to save sex until marriage, but to save all other foreplay until after the wedding as well. In addition to these physical commitments, emotional and spiritual commitments are also made to guard their hearts and minds against sexual compromise.

Boundaries on Thoughts and Words

One of the books I promote on these weekend retreats is *I Kissed Dating Goodbye,* by Joshua Harris. In the chapter called "Guard Your Heart," Josh writes of three pollutants to our hearts: infatuation, lust, and self-pity. While all three are certainly worth mentioning, I want to focus specifically on infatuation, because I feel that women's minds are particularly vulnerable to this pollutant:

> Infatuation—you've probably experienced it—the constant thoughts about someone who has caught your eye, the heart palpitations whenever that person walks by, the hours spent dreaming of a future with that special someone...
>
> Many of us have a difficult time seeing infatuation as potentially harmful. But we need to examine it carefully, because when you really think about it, infatuation can be a sinful response to attraction. Any time we allow someone to displace God as the focus of our affection, we've moved from innocent appreciation of someone's beauty or personality to the dangerous realm of infatuation. Instead of making God the object of our longing, we wrongly direct these feelings toward another human. We become idolaters, bowing to someone other than God, hoping that this person will meet our needs and bring fulfillment.
>
> God is righteously jealous for our hearts; after all, He has created us and redeemed us. He wants us to focus our thoughts, longings, and desires on Him. He lovingly blesses us with human relationships, but He first calls us to find our heart's delight in Him.[2]

I highly recommend reading this book, whether you are single or married. It will truly transform your mind regarding relationships and help you guide your children through the myriad of choices they'll make someday.

Another priceless treasure is Elizabeth Elliot's *Passion and Purity*. In a chapter entitled "What Women Do to Men," Elizabeth tells of the tragedy that occurs when women boldly pursue their potential mates. One woman explains in a letter to Elizabeth that after committing the matter to the Lord, she eventually dealt with the situation by "tactfully making her feelings known" to a young man to whom she became attached. After months of letters and phone calls, she was confused as to why this man wasn't reciprocating and why he was responding so coldly to her efforts. Elizabeth comments,

> Poor girl. She had no business in the first place "tactfully" making her feelings known. Poor choice of words. A woman taking that kind of initiative is not tactful. Very likely she scuttled any chances she might have had with the man. When he did not reply, she had a clear signal that he was not interested. To continue to try to arouse his interest by writing and calling was worse than useless.[3]

When it comes to potentially romantic relationships, we often need a muzzle over our mouths. Women like to talk about everything, get it all out in the open, make decisions, and get things done. But this is one area where you need to relinquish your control. Be still and know that He is God (Psalm 46:10), and that He will bestow favor and honor and withhold no good thing from those whose walk is blameless (Psalm 84:11).

Passion is Like Fire

What words would you use to describe a fire in a fireplace? Warm? Cozy? Romantic? Mesmerizing? Now, what are the words you would use to describe a fire raging on a mountainside? Dangerous? Destructive? Consuming? Out of control?

What is the difference between a fire in a fireplace and a fire raging on a mountainside? The fire we enjoy has boundaries around it. The fire that can destroy us has no boundaries. We can enjoy healthy relationships as long as we maintain healthy boundaries. Without those boundaries, relationships can consume us as quickly as a fire raging on a mountainside.

One exercise I recommend prior to entering any type of relationship is to make a chart similar to this one:

Acquaintances	Friendship	Group Dating	Courtship	Engagement	Marriage

Now, review the following list and determine for yourself at what stage in a relationship each intimate act is allowable. As silly as some of them may sound, all of them *are* intimate. Our society has desensitized us to the point that we often don't recognize intimacy when we experience it. As you categorize each act, remember that your focus should be to adopt God's standards for your behavior and refuse to be guided by the world's standards.

Eye-to-body contact
Eye-to-eye contact
Voice-to-voice contact—Public
Voice-to-voice contact—Private (i.e., phone conversations)
Conversations about your future
Conversations about emotional matters
Conversations about spiritual matters
Conversations about relational matters
Praying together as a couple
Holding hands momentarily
Holding hands for extended periods
Side or A-frame hug
Full body hug or bear hug*
Arm around shoulder
Arm around waist
Sitting on lap*
Light kiss or a peck (a mother kiss)
Strong kiss (head-to-head combat)
Deep, passionate kiss (tonsil hockey)*
Touching breasts**
Touching genitals**
Oral Sex**
Intercourse**

* Consider saving these, (and possibly others as well), until marriage.

** These should be exclusive to a marriage relationship.

Once you have mapped out your own personal boundaries using this exercise, write them in stone (on paper) and refer back to them often as a reminder to pace your levels of intimacy and to keep yourself pure in every stage of your relationships.

Boundary Mistakes

When I first became aware of my struggle with love addiction, I knew I had to set some boundaries in stone and stick to them, in order to remain faithful to the husband that God had blessed me with. Creating the physical boundaries was the easy part, but they soon proved to be insufficient. Once I had set my physical boundaries, God began showing me how they must evolve to include firmer emotional boundaries. Why? Because my struggle wasn't with the physical—my struggle was with the emotional. My boundaries needed to evolve so that I could avoid the outside emotional connections I often craved.

Avoidance of physical unfaithfulness would be easy once emotional unfaithfulness was no longer an issue. Originally, I had thought, "As long as I do not let another man touch me, I can be faithful." But out of ignorance, I continued to keep my heart out on my sleeve where it was vulnerable, and I soon learned that I could not separate my heart from my body for long. Once I had allowed my heart to be manipulated and my emotional sobriety to be lost, my body became a prime target.

I had to re-evaluate my boundaries to include much more than just the physical. I began to question every thought, word, and deed, and to measure it against what the Holy Spirit was revealing to me. Questions flooded my mind, such as, "What about hugs? Telephone conversations? How should I handle it when a guy stares at me? Was it ever okay to be alone with a man at all?" I needed to sort through all of these things and have a ready defense for when they happened; or better yet, learn how to be on the offensive to ensure they didn't happen in the first place.

The first time I had this revelation was several years ago, when I began receiving unsolicited phone calls from a married male friend within our church congregation. I recognized that these private phone conversations were an emotional connection waiting to happen. I told my husband about these calls and asked him, "Is there anything that I have done or said that would lead him to believe that I invite his calls?" Greg replied, "Not to my knowledge, but the hugs you give him every time you see him at church could be misinterpreted."

"But I hug *everybody* at church!" I retorted.

"Maybe you should be more discerning about who you hug and how you hug them!" was his honest and loving response. And he couldn't have been more right. Be aware that guys are not only stimulated visually, but also by touch. Hugging a man every time you see him may be sending him a signal that you don't want to send. If a hug is called for, at an appropriate time, in an appropriate place, with an appropriate person, give a side hug or an A-frame hug—never a full body hug or a bear hug. The key is to use discernment in who you hug, when you hug, how you hug, and why you hug. A good rule is not to make hugging a habit, and to avoid physical touch when it is not necessarily called for.

Another boundaries mistake that I've made is thinking that having lunch with a man is okay as long as we are in a public place. Eating with someone, as odd as it may sound, is an intimate experience, especially if there is no one else at the table with you. There have been many inappropriate conversations take place in crowded restaurants, and plenty of affairs between co-workers started by taking lunch breaks together. Going out to eat together is something that a couple would normally do on a date, so realize that your cooperation in dining alone with someone could lead them to believe that you are not just a lunch partner, but a lunch *date*.

Boundaries Continue Evolving

While I was contemplating what other healthy boundaries I should incorporate, I heard a male counselor speaking at a conference on emotional boundaries. Not only did he refuse to dine alone with a female, but he took this one step further to say that he would not be alone in a car with a woman other than his mother, wife, or daughter. "Being alone in a car provides the opportunity for intimate conversations. If a woman needs to ride with me, I make sure a third person comes along." Adopting this boundary as well has helped me distance myself even from the temptation to engage in intimate conversations with a man.

Another boundary I've incorporated within the past few years is that I do not have one-on-one "closed door" meetings with male co-workers. At first, I was afraid this action would be offensive to men, or that they would think I was strange. However, no one has ever questioned why I leave the door open or bring a co-worker into the office with me when meeting with a man. I think that in this day and age of sexual harassment lawsuits flying, such "open door" policies are respected and appreciated by honorable men.

Another personal boundary of mine is that I refuse to go out of my way to run into or converse with a man. It isn't becoming of a lady when it is obvious that she hungers for his attention. My motto is, "When en route, stay on course!" In other words, don't go the long way to the bathroom because you'll get to pass by *his* desk. If his desk happens to be along the shortest way to the bathroom, then don't hesitate to take the long way if he is a distraction from your focus on your work or on the Lord.

If you are en route somewhere and coincidentally run into an object of temptation (a true coincidence, not a planned one), know that the Lord has trusted that your paths can come together and you will behave in a way that gives Him glory. Consider these chance encounters a test. Every temptation is. According to Max Lucado, temptation is a two-sided coin. It will make you weak enough to fall or strong enough to stand. If you have to stop and make up some excuse to gain a morsel of attention, then obviously you are weak enough to fall. Such acting out doesn't say much about your intimate relationship with Jesus fulfilling you completely, does it?

Boundary Examples from Scripture

The majority of the Book of Genesis (Chapters 37–50) is devoted to the incredible story of a godly young man named Joseph. If you recall, Joseph was the favored son of Jacob and Rachel, and received a colorful coat as a gift from his loving father (signifying favor and a position of power over the rest of his brothers). Joseph had experienced dreams of his brothers bowing down to him, and he made the mistake of sharing those dreams with them, as jealous as they already were. So, at the first opportunity, Joseph's brothers captured him, stripped him of his coat, and threw him into a pit. They were going to kill him, but Joseph's brother Judah suggested they sell him as a slave instead. Thus, when a caravan of Ishmaelites came along on their way to Egypt, Joseph was sold for twenty shekels of silver. Upon arrival in Egypt, Joseph was then sold to Potiphar, one of Pharoah's officials and the captain of the guard (Genesis 37).

Joseph found great favor in the eyes of Potiphar, and was entrusted with many responsibilities. He brought even greater prosperity to Potiphar and eventually was trusted with everything in both the house and in the field, with the exception of the food Potiphar ate and Potiphar's wife. In Genesis 39:6–10, we gain insight into Joseph's character as we read:

> *Now Joseph was well built and handsome, and after a while his master's wife took notice of Joseph and said, "Come to bed with me!"*

*But he refused. "With me in charge," he told her, "my master does not concern himself with anything in the house; everything he owns he has entrusted to my care. No one is greater in this house than I am. My master has withheld nothing from me except you, because you are his wife. How then could I do such a wicked thing and sin against God?" And though she spoke to Joseph day after day, he refused to go to bed with her **or even be with her*** (emphasis added).

The story continues with many intriguing twists and turns, but the point I want to make about Joseph's character is that he was a man of integrity and honor. Not only could he refuse the sexual advances of a beautiful woman, he was smart enough *not to even be with her* (v. 10). Joseph knew that both physical and emotional boundaries were necessary to protect him from such a sin. Knowing this woman would try to wear him down over time, Joseph refused to even be around her so that his resolve would not become weak. The concept I want you to grasp is that there is no shame in running away from temptation!

Running away is exactly what King David should have done, but unfortunately his story leans the opposite direction. In 2 Samuel 11:2–5 we read:

One evening, David got up from his bed and walked around on the roof of the palace. From the roof he saw a woman bathing. The woman was very beautiful, and David sent someone to find out about her. The man said, "Isn't this Bathsheba, the daughter of Eliam and the wife of Uriah the Hittite? Then David sent messengers to get her. She came to him, and he slept with her. Then she went back home. The woman conceived and sent word to David, saying, "I am pregnant."

This story continues on with many intriguing twists and turns as well, but in a different way. Once David had committed adultery with Uriah's wife, he sank even deeper in sin when he tried to cover everything up. When his cover-up plot failed, he resorted to having Uriah moved to the front lines of battle so that he would be killed. As consequences of his sin, the son born to David and Bathsheba would die, and David's other sons would also commit the sins of adultery and murder, bringing further shame on the king's family.

One weak, self-indulgent moment turned into a living nightmare for David, and it only takes one moment of weakness for our lives to turn into a nightmare as well. Sin only festers and grows and gives birth to both spiritual and physical death. However, no sin is so great that our repentance is not accepted by our merciful God. Although there were grave consequences to his sin, the repentant David still went down in biblical history as a man after God's own heart.

As we become more intentional about building and maintaining our own personal boundaries (both emotional and physical), we will find that the temptation to sin sexually holds no power over us, as we may have believed in the past. As we refuse to be in the presence of our stumbling blocks and stay away from the rooftops where temptation awaits us, we will also prove ourselves to be honorable servants of our Lord and women after God's own heart.

QUESTIONS FOR INTROSPECTION:

- What were the "pet baby alligator" sins of your past (seemingly innocent ones) that made you vulnerable to Satan's attack?

- Are there any "pet baby alligator" sins remaining in your life that could still drag you under someday?

- What new boundaries need to be established to prevent this from happening?

- How do you define a healthy physical boundary in a relationship? What are your physical boundaries prior to marriage? (Or, if you are married, what are your boundaries with other men?)

- Moving beyond the physical, how do you define healthy emotional, mental, and spiritual boundaries in a premarital (or extramarital) relationship?

- How can you guard your heart against infatuation and emotional affairs?

• Is there anyone in your life who poses such a threat to your emotional control that you should refuse to even be in his presence?

• How will you know when you are getting dangerously close to the edge of Satan's pit?

• Even though you may have fallen into that pit before, do you believe yourself still to be a woman after God's own heart? Why or why not?

CHAPTER ELEVEN

A Heavenly Affair

Show the wonder of Your great love, You who save by
Your right hand those who take refuge in You from their foes.
Keep me as the apple of Your eye; hide me in
the shadow of Your wings...
—PSALM 17:7–8

Before we look at discovering a heavenly affair with Jesus Christ, let us examine God's will for His beloved as it relates to our past, our present, and our future. Jesus Christ is the same yesterday, today, and forever (Hebrews 13:8), and it is important for us to realize that His will for our lives is truly perfect.

Regarding the past, He has always wanted the very best for you. He has never failed to desperately desire an intimate relationship with you. He has been your biggest cheerleader and most loyal fan. The things that have broken your heart have shattered His. The things that have brought you tears have caused Him to sob bitterly. The things that have brought laughter in your life have caused Him to dance with joy. His hope is in us and He longs for our hope to be in Him. Realize, before you waste another day with your back turned, that God is *for* you and not *against* you. He's on our team and is most certainly the M.V.P. (most valuable player).

Regarding the present, know that it is God who has opened your eyes to these sex, love, and relationship issues with which you are dealing, and He longs to deliver you right now from your past and into your future. He doesn't want to wait another day to take back what the devil stole from you. He wants to restore your dignity and your self-worth. He wants to mend your broken heart and help you let go of all the bitterness that has weighed your heart down for years. He wants to give you a sense of release from your trespasses and help you gain the closure you've been aching for from your past. He wants to take your chin in His hand, lift your pretty head, gaze deep into your soul, and let you see your reflection as the apple of His eye.

And looking ahead to the future, do you have any idea what glorious things God has in store for you? Your mind isn't big enough to even begin to fathom the blessings awaiting you. Jeremiah 29:11–13 says,

> *For I know the plans that I have for you, **declares** the Lord, plans to prosper you and not to harm you, plans to give you hope and a future. Then you will call upon Me and come and pray to Me and I will listen to you. You will seek Me and find Me when you seek Me with all your heart* (emphasis added).

Did you catch that this passage isn't something the Lord "casually mentions"? It is something He *declares!*

But there is one hurdle you must leap over, and that is letting go of your disappointments in your past so you can triumph in the appointments God has in your future. If you are still facing your past, your back is to your future, and you will stumble into it as clumsily as you stumbled through your past temptations and sin. Again, repentance means turning around and going the opposite direction, and having repented of those sins, you now must literally turn around and *charge* toward all that God has for you in the future.

This hurdle may sound like it takes an enormous amount of strength to overcome. You may think that you don't possess such strength. You are right. You don't. But God does. And this process of moving triumphantly into your future is not about your renewed efforts to do what is right, but about your complete and total surrender and reliance upon God to intercede in your weakness and provide a supernatural amount of strength and power. You've been spiritually dead, and now you are looking to be resurrected into life. Human power won't do—you need resurrection power. And there are only two prerequisites to receiving God's power: *faith and trust.*

Leaving Our Comfort Zone

If ever there was an example in Scripture of one whose faith and trust gave him such a deep relationship with God that he had the power to abandon his past and move boldly into his future, it was Abraham. In Genesis 12, we see the Lord call to Abraham (then called Abram), "Leave your country, your people, and your father's household and go to the land I will show you."

You may have read that passage before and not thought much of it, but do you realize what faith and trust this seventy-five-year-old man must have had to leave his comfort zone—his home and the people that he loved—for no other reason except that God told him to? This involved a huge sacrifice. Couldn't you imagine his friends saying, "But *where* are you going, Abram? What will you do there? How will you and your family survive?" The only way Abram could respond to such questions was, "I don't know, but God does."

And he set out toward what God had for him in total obedience. He packed up his wife, his servants, his household, everything. He burned all bridges behind him and there would be no turning back. This type of total commitment is vital if we want to move toward all that God has for us. In Luke 14:33, Jesus said,

"...any of you who does not give up everything he has cannot be my disciple."

Abram's home, Haran, was filled with idolatry, and God wanted to separate Abram from it in order to deepen his faith in the one true God. Like Abram, we also live in a land filled with sin. A break must be made, habits broken, cultural patterns renounced. In the spiritual life, there can be no "receiving" without first "renouncing." Are you, like Abram, willing to leave anything behind in order to follow God to what He has for you?

The Great Rewards of Obedience

God wanted to bring Abram into a new land and a new way of life. What did God have for Abram as a reward for his obedience? In Genesis 12:2–3 God says to Abram,

> *I will make you into a great nation and I will bless you; I will make your name great, and you will be a blessing. I will bless those who bless you, and whoever curses you I will curse; and all the peoples on earth will be blessed through you.*

Did you hear that? Nothing but blessing! From that time forth God talked with Abraham, revealing Himself increasingly in an intimate relationship as One who loved Abraham and would be his shield. He promised Abraham a new land that would be passed down through a multitude of generations. He made his name great as the "father" of nations (the original chosen one of the Jewish faith; the patriarch of the bloodline of Christ).

In Genesis 15:3–4, we also see that God gave Abraham the desire of his heart—a son born to his wife, Sarah, when Abraham was 100 years old. But the greatest blessing Abraham received is the exact blessing that we stand to receive as well. In Genesis 15:1, the Lord came to Abraham in a vision and said, "*I am your very great reward.*" Of all that Abraham was given as a reward for his obedience, what could possibly be greater than the deepest relationship possible with God?

Yes, God wants to bless your socks off, too! *He* is *your* very great reward (one that surpasses any blessing you could possibly imagine). God has promised to make you a blessing to your family, your church, your friends, your neighborhood, your country, etc. for many generations to come. This is both your inheritance and your calling.

Opening God's Love Letter to You

How do we become a blessing to others? Start with blessing the Lord by reading the love letter He wrote to you.

"Ooh! God wrote *me* a love letter?" you say with your heart all aflutter? Yes, He did. It is called the Holy Bible. In this love letter, He explains to you the mysteries of creation and the beginning of His family tree in Genesis. He reveals Himself as our deliverer in Exodus. He inspires us with sonnets in the Psalms. He graces us with wisdom in the Proverbs. He romances us in Song of Solomon. He foretells of our Savior's coming in the Books of the Prophets. He gives us a personal autobiography of our Lover in the Gospels. He teaches us how to live righteously in Paul's letters. And He promises His eminent return in Revelation.

The list could go on and on of the gifts He has given us in Scripture, but my words will not illuminate Scripture for you. The Bible is like a wrapped gift directly from your Heavenly Father. You must unwrap it and look at what is inside, in order to be delighted by His thoughtfulness in giving you such a blessing. Go search for what God has waiting for you there and read it as if it truly were God's love letter to you—because it is!

I was originally intimidated by Scripture, and perhaps you are, too. There seemed to be so many pages and such little time to invest trying to put them all together in such a way that I could ever understand it, or imagine how it applied to me. But through my struggle to overcome love addiction, I discovered this truth:

The Bible will either keep you from sin,
or sin will keep you from the Bible.

I had to turn to God's Word to help me keep my head on straight from day to day as I tried desperately to avoid emotional affairs. I started by reading on my own, but got frustrated because it seemed like trying to put a huge jigsaw puzzle together without the box-top picture to go by. Soon afterwards (in God's sovereignty), I was required to take an Old Testament History class in college. I was amazed at how applicable the stories were to today, and how richly characters were illustrated and brought to life. It was better than any novel I'd ever read, so I also signed up for a New Testament Principles class. That is when I was blown away at the magnitude of all that the Bible had to say. It was full of comfort, hope, peace, encouragement, correction, compassion, and motivation. Soon after, I registered for a Major World Religions class at a community college, so I could compare my faith with what others believed. I was ecstatic to come out of that class knowing that I was on the winning team.

No other religion in the world offers the concept of *grace*. In all other religions, salvation must be earned by avoiding evil deeds and practicing good ones all the time. If you are thinking that is impossible, you are right! Only in Christianity is one saved regardless of their ability to consistently avoid evil and do good. We are not only saved from hell by what Christ did for us on the cross to remove our transgressions, but we are also empowered by the Holy Spirit to help us avoid sin and practice the good things God inspires us to do.

After graduation from college, I still hungered for greater revelations of God's Word. The more Scripture you take in, the more you crave it. So I became active in Bible Study Fellowship (BSF

International) and spent two years dissecting and devouring John's Gospel and Genesis. Other tools that I've found beneficial to my study are Henry Blackaby's *Experiencing God* Bible Study (Lifeway Press), Walk Thru the Bible's *Daily Walk* Magazine, and *The One-Year Chronological Bible* (Harvest House Publishers), which has all of Scripture arranged in the order that the events actually happened.

I say all of this to inspire you not to simply depend on your own understanding of Scripture if you are new to Bible study. Find a good commentary or workbook to guide you and explain things as you go along. Even if you grew up in the church, as I did, acknowledging your elementary understanding of the things you have heard from Scripture is an invitation for God to begin taking you to higher levels of understanding. The writer of Hebrews 5:11–14 warns the people against falling away from God and states,

> *We have much to say about this, but it is hard to explain because you are slow to learn. In fact, though by this time you ought to be teachers, you need someone to teach you the elementary truths of God's word all over again. You need milk, not solid food! Anyone who lives on milk, being still an infant, is not acquainted with the teaching about righteousness. But solid food is for the mature, who by constant use have trained themselves to distinguish good from evil.*

As you acquaint yourself to the teachings about righteousness and begin to apply them (there is a big difference between "knowing" them and "applying" them), you will see truth after truth revealed to you. In time, you will gain understanding, confidence and an appreciation of how the Holy Spirit can bring enlightenment to the hearts and minds of those who truly seek to know God. Although the Bible may have seemed like a collection of irrelevant stories and cold words from the past, expressing your faith and trust and committing to study God's love letter to you will bring "revelation knowledge," whereby you won't just *read* it, you will *live* it. You will soon find that God truly appears to us through Scripture. Verse after verse will begin to take on personal meaning, and you will be inspired to rightfully claim promise after promise.

Conversations With Your Lover

Remember how eager you used to be for the phone to ring? You waited anxiously and even picked up the receiver several times to make sure the phone was working. You couldn't wait to talk to that special guy. Then when it finally did ring, you were so disappointed to hear Aunt Sally's voice on the other end.

How would you like to experience the excitement of having your lover ring the phone off the wall all day, every day? Would that make you feel special? My friend, God has had your number memorized since the day you were born and has been calling for years, but you've been on the other line talking to some *Joe Schmoe* or *Chuck Shmuck*. Break that connection and make the connection your heart is really longing for!

What connection am I talking about? *Prayer.* It means "having a conversation with God," but many of us have grown up with a "Santa Claus" mentality of God and we only go to Him with our wish lists. We go to God in prayer to tell Him that we want something, or that we have this special need. But what about simply talking to Him about how your day is going? Sharing your thoughts and feelings? Telling Him of your adoration? Confessing your shortcomings? Venting your frustrations with Him? Thanking Him for your many blessings? Dreaming about your future in His presence and asking Him to guide your visions?

Remember when you were a young teenager how often you would talk to your best friend? You called each other in the morning to see what the other one was wearing to school. You met right after breakfast to walk to campus together. You found each other at lunch and sat together religiously. If you shared any of the same classes, the teacher had to separate you for talking and even then, you found a way to pass notes back and forth. Then you went home after school and talked for hours on the phone, as if you hadn't seen each other all day. And what did you do with your weekends? You hung out at your best friend's house!

What would have happened if you had gone for several days—even weeks or months—without contacting her? Chances are, you wouldn't have that best friend anymore. You would drift away from her and find other relationships to satisfy you. Well, that is what happens when you go for days or weeks or months without talking and sharing with God. Oh, He doesn't go anywhere... *you* are the one who moves away. You break His heart with your independence, and you miss out on all that He has to say and show to you.

Feeling convicted? If so, take refuge in the fact that, regardless of how long it has been since you talked and enjoyed fellowship of God, you are always a welcome sight on His doorstep! Don't let the fact that it has been so long keep you from running back and crawling into His lap today. You have so much to lose by letting pride keep you from humbly returning to God in prayer. You have so much to gain by restoring that connection with Him. John 14:13–14 says, "And I will do whatever you ask in My name, so that the Son may bring glory to the Father. You may ask Me for anything in My name, and I will do it." What an incredible promise! We've wanted to hear a man offer us anything our hearts desired for years, but Jesus is the only one who can make this promise *and* fulfill it!

Don't know where to start? Begin by praying some of the Scripture that you read, such as the Lord's Prayer (Matthew 6:9–13), or the Prayer of Jabez (1 Chronicles 4:10). Coupling Scripture with prayer is like a one-two punch against Satan's schemes. When you pray using the divine inspiration of God's own words, you are bound to have them answered. One of my favorite passages of Scripture to pray is Psalm 51:10–15:

Create in me a pure heart, O God, and renew a steadfast spirit within me. Do not cast me from Your presence or take Your Holy Spirit from me. Restore to me the joy of Your salvation and grant me a willing spirit to sustain me. Then I will teach transgressors Your ways, and sinners will turn back to You. Save me from bloodguilt, O God, the God who saves me, and my tongue will sing of Your righteousness. O Lord, open my lips, and my mouth will declare Your praise.

Scheduling Your Rendezvous

Conversing with God is like conversing with anyone else—you need to find the time and a place. Make a special time—a time when you can completely focus your attention on Him. My favorite time each day is on my morning walks. I used to walk with girlfriends, but not anymore. This is my one hour of uninterrupted time to walk and talk with God alone. After twenty or thirty minutes of my rambling on and on, I usually hear Him say, "Be sure to leave some time to listen, too. I've got a lot I want to say to you today." I'm glad He reminds me! I previously used my prayer time to tell God everything I thought He needed to know (as if He didn't already), but I've learned that it is in listening that my heart overflows with the sweet sentiments He whispers into my ear. I've sometimes been awakened at five a.m., hearing God whisper in my ear, "Get up! Come and spend time with Me! I'm dying to talk to you!" How could I ever sleep through such an intimate invitation?

Finding a special place to meet with Him is like coordinating a rendezvous spot! Thoughtfully consider a unique place where every time you pass by it, you feel God calling you into His arms. For me, this used to be a great big overstuffed chair, but I found I'd fall asleep too easily. Then I set up an "altar" in the corner of my bedroom, with a lace cloth, a small candle, a cross, special mementos that reminded me of people I needed to pray for, and "souvenirs" from special places or events that God and I had shared together. This is a great idea—if you don't have a cat who loves to try to climb lace cloths, knock over tables, and bat trinkets all around the house with her paws.

Now my special places are in our pine forest where God and I walk and talk together, on the balcony porch swing where we can watch the sunset together, or on the rug in my study where I have often planted my face and sought His divine inspiration and perseverance while writing. You'll find your own special places and special times. Custom tailor them and give God your absolute best block of time each day in a quiet place away from distractions. Then your rendezvous with your Lover will be the most anxiously awaited part of your day!

Praise, Worship and Meditation

Again, entire books have been written on all of these subjects of Scripture reading, prayer, praise, worship, and meditation, and I don't pretend to even do any of them justice here. But my desire is for the Holy Spirit to take my few words of expression about their importance and impress them on your heart, to the point that you hunger and thirst for these things, for they truly bring life!

Praise and worship are also a vital part of our love relationship with the Lord. I'm not talking about going to church, although that is certainly a part of it. I'm talking about expressing your deepest devotion to and appreciation of the Lord for who He is and what He means to you. Again, you can begin with Scripture if you need a jump-start. The Bible tells how God is our Rock, our Redeemer, our Salvation, our Refuge, our Strength, our Deliverer, our Father, our Friend, and the list goes on and on.

Every time you read a passage that gives you new insight into God's character, stop and praise Him for that special attribute. If you find yourself at a loss for what to say or do in your praise and worship times, simply do whatever comes naturally. God will appreciate whatever you have to offer if it is offered as a heartfelt expression. I am reminded of this when my precious son brings me amateur drawings to hang on my refrigerator. It isn't the skill or the expertise that matters to the recipient, it is the love and the passion which inspired it that makes it a true *work of heart*.

Expressing our love to God through praise and worship over and over should never feel redundant. I've heard the story of a couple going in for counseling, complaining of a dying marriage. The wife whines, "He never tells me he loves me!" Her husband informs the counselor, "I told her I loved her the day we got married, and that I'd let her know if anything changed!" A pretty sad excuse for a love relationship, huh? Well, think of praise and worship as merely our way of regularly saying to God, "I love You!" Tell Him as often as you think of Him, and know that as you worship Him in such a private way, you are delighting His heart. What could be more satisfying than knowing that you are a delight to the very heart of God?

When you read of God's attributes and understand more and more about His character, you will most certainly fall more deeply head over heels in love with Him! You'll no longer be able to read about Him, shut your Bible, and go on about your day. You will be transformed by the knowledge of what God is like. Be sure to write down your special revelations that God gives you of Himself. Start a journal of these precious nuggets. Tape meaningful passages of Scripture on your bathroom mirror so that you'll see them every morning. Write them down on an index card to carry around in your purse all day, so that every time you put on lipstick, you'll remember to give praise to the Lord with those lips.

This is what is meant by "meditating" on God's Word. In essence, it is like "chewing" on it all day long, rather than just taking a bite and spitting it out after your quiet time is over. If you want to digest it and allow it to nourish you, then you have to chew on it. When it finally digests, you'll begin to crave another of God's morsels, and another. You'll become so addicted to learning about God and meditating on His Word that He will be your all-consuming thought. And when He consumes your thoughts, it is much easier not to be distracted by petty temptations.

Not Rules, But a Relationship

What I have presented here is not intended to be a "formula" for how to have a real Christian experience. I'm not saying that if you read your Bible, pray, etc., that you will become super-spiritual and nothing will ever bother you. I concur with Dr. Gary Collins as he writes in *The Biblical Basis of Christian Counseling for People Helpers*:

> It is true that the Christian life can be a struggle (Ephesians 6:12) but spiritual growth is not a performance-driven, success-oriented push for some victorious super-spirituality. Salvation came because of the mercy and grace of God, and spiritual growth comes in the same way. We don't need works, ecstatic experiences, self-flagellation, special Spirit baptisms, spiritual twelve-step programs or anything else to bring true spirituality. Christ's work on the cross is necessary and sufficient for both the new birth and Christian maturity. Both depend on what Christ has done and is doing in the lives of people who have faith in Him. In the Bible, salvation refers to a growth process that begins with the new birth but continues throughout life as Christ molds us and makes us more like Him. We can resist the growth process, of course, or we can get distracted by our own efforts to perform and to reach spiritual success. But real growth comes only when we consistently and humbly submit to Christ, admit our weaknesses and sinfulness, and recognize the emptiness of efforts to reach spiritual maturity on our own.[1]

Everything in your life—everything about forgetting your past, everything about finding peace at present, everything about having confidence in your future—is completely dependent upon your love relationship with God. If your love relationship with God isn't right, nothing in your life will be right. Believe me, I've tried it both ways, and so have thousands of women I've talked to over the past decade of ministry.

Each time a woman confesses her current struggles with sexual temptation, I eventually ask her to describe things such as her quiet time, her prayer life, or her moments of worship. These women often scramble and search for a response, if they come up with one at all. But those women who report victory in their lives over this struggle with unhealthy relationships always have a ready response because they do not have to make one up.

The overcomers are truly those who are deeply involved in a love relationship with Jesus and are reading His love letters over and over, calling Him up every day and several times a day, telling Him how crazy they are about Him, and waiting on Him to see how they can serve Him. What overcomers have discovered through their experiences is that, as much as we have all longed for intimacy, it cannot truly be found in human relationships to the full extent that we crave it.

Why? The word *intimacy* can best be understood by breaking it down into its syllables: "*in-to-me—see.*" Intimacy is the ability to see what is actually on the inside of someone, to minister to that person accordingly, and to provide what their heart most desperately needs and desires. And can any man on the planet actually do that? No! Who is the only One who can truly see what is inside of you? The God who made you. The God who knit you together in your mother's womb also holds the secret formula to fulfill your heart's desires and to satisfy you in an inexplicable way.

The Overcomer's Path

God does not want you or any other woman to continue down a path toward destruction through emotional idolatry or sexual immorality. He loved you while you were involved in those things, but He loves you too much to leave you there. He longs to derail you from your fast track to relational misery. He has a better road for you to travel—one that leads to prosperity and hope (Jeremiah 29:11); contentment (1 Timothy 6:6); comfort (Psalms 46:1–3); courage and strength (Isaiah 40:29); real love, joy, peace, patience, kindness, goodness, gentleness, faithfulness, and self-control (Galatians 5:22). This, my friend, is the overcomer's path. It leads to eternal life and riches in glory.

While on this path, you will travel swiftly some days and be sluggish on others. You will not be exempt from the human pot-holes of weariness and temptation. You will have to work hard to remain traveling down this road, and there will be many days when you will want to say, "Hey! I deserve a break today!" It is on those days that Satan will strategically place a detour in your path, with a Popsicle stand on the side of that road. And guess what? That Popsicle stand is going to have your favorite flavor. Yes, Satan knows your taste for sin, and he'll try everything he can to get you, like Eve, to take a bite of something forbidden.

Our only hope of staying on this road toward righteous living is to learn to separate our will from our emotions. Billy Graham preaches about the "emotion train," where you let your emotions rule your decisions and your will is at the caboose, following wherever the emotion engine leads. We need to put our emotions at the caboose and our will at the engine, so that we can be driven by our decision to live righteously regardless of how easy it is or how good it feels. Then, when we hear our emotions saying, "But I've worked hard! I'm tired! I deserve a break today!" your "will engine" can keep you on track and continue to pull you in the right direction.

It is easier to *act* your way into a new way of feeling than to *feel* your way into a new way of acting. How can your will take precedence over your emotions? When temptation strikes, in the words of Elizabeth Elliot, you merely "do the next thing." When you are on your way to the laundromat and you pass by his house and hear your emotions scream, "Stop! I need a break!" you simply keep driving and go do your laundry. When you are about to cook dinner and the thought of calling him pops into your mind, you merely proceed to the stove and start cooking. I've been practicing this simple principle for years, and "doing the next thing" each day can add up to a lifetime of obedience. It is through this daily obedience that we live the overcoming life, which is our inheritance through Christ Jesus.

> *To* [her] *who overcomes, I will give the right to sit with Me on my throne, just as I overcame and sat down with My Father on His throne* (Revelation 3:21).

 QUESTIONS FOR INTROSPECTION:

• How open are you to leaving your comfort zone and going wherever God leads you, even if it means leaving many relationships behind?

• What do you envision being the greatest reward for your obedience? Is the deepest relationship possible with God enough of an incentive for you?

- What has your impression of the Bible been in the past? Have you read much of it?

- What hinders you from devouring God's love letter to you? How can those hindrances be overcome?

- Do you have regular conversations with your Lover (Jesus), or do you leave Him waiting by the phone for days on end?

- What rendezvous spot can you imagine being the place where you meet God face-to-face each day?

- What blocks of quality time can you carve out of each day in anticipation of true intimacy with God?

- What other creative ways can you express your heartfelt love for Jesus Christ?

CHAPTER TWELVE

A Well Woman

"If you repent, I will restore you that you may serve me;
if you utter worthy, not worthless, words,
you will be my spokesman."
—JEREMIAH 15:19

As we've explored our thirst for love and intimacy and learned that only Christ can truly satisfy us, you've more than likely thought of many others who desperately need to hear this message. Most women, still whirled by the world's view of sex, love, romance, and relationships, would say exactly what we have said before—"I'm not a love *addict*, I'd just like to know more about this topic."

Yet, as we explored, we often discovered some of our deepest, darkest truths. As we sought to learn how to help others, we recognized our own need for help first. As much as we thought that our patterns of relating to men were par for the course as far as the world's standards go, we came to realize that those are not the standards that we want to live by. No, to continue looking for love in all the wrong places would prove excruciatingly painful, and we recognized the danger involved to ourselves and to our future partners.

These futile thoughts and behaviors are as dangerous as any

other compulsive addiction. Many emotional or sexual affairs, stalkings, suicides, murders, and crimes of passion are a direct result of our insatiable thirst for love and intimacy. Our culture has traditionally glorified this addiction, promoting the idea that someday we will all fall in love and live happily ever after. We have finally recognized that this fantasy fails to mention the enormous ongoing investment that relationships truly require.

No, our lives would not unfold as they do in the movies or in romance novels. If they did, the endings would also be as tragic. We long for something more real, more genuine, more deep, more lasting. We long for true intimacy, and recognize that such can never be found in the places where we've typically searched. Rather than continuing to look in the same places expecting to find different results, we've put a halt to this insanity. Finally, rather than looking to creation, we have discovered the joy of falling in love with our Creator, and now anticipate the blessings that will come from living happily ever after in His arms.

So great is our satisfaction in our discovery that we can't possibly keep such a good thing to ourselves. No, our burden is for the multitude of other women who are still looking for love in all the wrong places and choking on stagnant water, unaware of the living water that Christ freely offers.

Discovering Your Oasis

Imagine for a moment that you and thousands of other women have been living in a scorching desert for quite some time. Each of you has been wandering about, desperately seeking water for as long as you can remember, but all anyone has ever found is sand. Every woman is parched, many are dehydrated, some on the verge of death. By chance, you alone catch a glimpse of an oasis on the horizon.

"Could it be a mirage?" you wonder, and you run with reckless abandon toward your only hope for survival. Yes! This is a gushing spring with cool water flowing briskly. You kneel in the blazing sand, cup your hands, splash the cool water across your parched lips and feel the moisture flow across your tongue and down your throat. You plunge your face deep and slurp as hard and fast as you can. Your thirst is finally quenched. You set up camp permanently beside this spring, knowing that it is the hope of all your tomorrows.

Now, would you possibly consider keeping this spring to yourself? Could you keep this oasis a secret from the other dying women? Knowing that there is no chance of them using it all up because its source is eternal, could you live with yourself knowing that you could have shared this hope with them and prevented them from perishing, and yet chose not to?

Of course not. You would be so anxious to spread the news about this water you had found. You would grab unbelieving women by the hand and drag them to the spring. You would coax them into the water and splash them with its cool drops, convincing them that this is no mirage—this is the real thing! And you'd invite them to set up camp beside you and share this life-giving source, right?

Well, sister, I pray that you have in fact discovered the real thing. I pray that the love which has eluded you, relationship after relationship, is finally a reality in your life because of your new-found knowledge of Christ's unconditional and eternal love for you. I pray that the stagnant water that earthly men have to offer would pale in comparison to the living water that has finally quenched your thirsty soul!

A Quick Refresher

Let's celebrate this victory by briefly recapping all that we have learned over the past twelve chapters. First, we recognized the neon signs that made us targets for unhealthy attention and we died to ourselves so that Christ could live in us. We embraced

God's liberating love for us and went back to the blueprints to understand what God intended when He created men, women, sex, and love. We recognized the sin dwelling in our own hearts that had led us to distorting God's perfect plan for our sexuality, and we confessed and repented from that sin. We removed the scarlet letter from our chest, refusing to become a self-fulfilling prophecy to the labels many had placed on us. We invited Jesus Christ to perfect us and continue transforming us into His likeness. We examined those whom we had sinned against and asked God, as well as those we hurt, when appropriate, for forgiveness. We released all bitterness and anger toward those who had sinned against us. We allowed God to show us better boundaries to live by, and have begun investing ourselves in a heavenly affair rather than a worldly one.

Do you realize that we are now walking miracles? Where we once felt isolated and detached, we have made real connections to God and hopefully to other women. Our inner rage over our lack of nurturing or early abandonment has melted into a sense of peace and forgiveness. Where we were once highly manipulative and controlling of others, we now focus on self-control and extend grace to others. Where we once thought we needed relational roller-coaster rides and emotional attachments like we needed food and water, we now possess discernment and power to deny our flesh when necessary and live by the Spirit. Where we once possessed an insatiable appetite for attention and affection, our only insatiable appetite now is our hunger for the Lord.

No longer do we mistake intensity for intimacy. No longer do we confuse sexual attraction with true love. We've abandoned our "double life." We no longer require a relationship with a man to feel complete. We are confident in our roles as daughters of the King and the brides of Christ. We are no longer victims, but victors. We are no longer Women at the Well, but *Well Women!* Give God the glory for the healing He has brought to your past, the joy

He has brought to your present, and the hope He has given you for your future!

Discovering a New Compassion

Now, what will happen as you walk through this world as a Well Woman? You are going to have a new insight into other women who need healing. You will be able to see it in how they dress. You'll recognize the neon sign on their forehead. Their countenance will exude a need for attention, and you will want to attend to them in a way that no man will ever be able to. You will want to share your living water with them.

This new drive you have toward these other Women at the Well is called *compassion*. It is a gift from God; He gives it to you so that you can be His hands and feet, words and actions. You now possess the heart and the mind of Christ. You now share His thoughts and His heartbeat, and your heart will literally break for these women as you recognize them. The reason that He saved you is so that you would then turn around and help Him save others. It's not that God *needs* us, but He *chooses* to work through us. It is called a "chain of grace." Don't be the weak link in that chain!

In 2 Corinthians 1:3–4, Paul writes,

> *Praise be to the God and Father of our Lord Jesus Christ, the Father of compassion and the God of all comfort, who comforts us in all our troubles **so that we can comfort those in any trouble with the comfort we ourselves have received from God*** (emphasis added).

Share your miraculous testimony with other women and you, too, can experience the incredible blessing of being an incredible blessing to someone else. In the words of T.D. Jakes:

> *The point of your greatest misery is also*
> *the point of your greatest ministry.*

I recall going to a baseball game while I was still in counseling for these issues. I noticed that I was no longer looking around to see who was checking me out. Instead, I found myself observing the other women, and watching *them* look around to see who was checking them out. I could literally sit there in the stands and pick out the women who were love addicts. I could see the same neon sign on their foreheads that I once wore. This may sound judgmental, but I wasn't doing this for the purpose of condemnation. Instead of "people-watching," I was "soul-watching," and God was showing me who was in need of prayer.

Interceding for them is sometimes the only thing we can do. I would never dream of approaching a stranger out of nowhere with, "Hey! You are a love addict! I can tell by watching you!" That would be no way to win friends and influence people. We must heed the words of Dr. John Maxwell when he says, "People don't care how much you know until they know how much you care!"

Planting a Seed

While there will be many times that intercessory prayer is your only available course of action, there will be other prime moments that you have a brief window of opportunity to go a little deeper. It is then that you not only pray, but also throw out a line to see if she will bite! For example, one day I was standing in line at the grocery store. The clerk was an attractive woman in her mid-thirties, and she was carrying on a normal conversation with me. Suddenly, a handsome boy about half her age bolted up behind her and handed her a key. She turned to face him, lit up like a Christmas tree, and lost all awareness of anyone else being in the store. "Thanks!" she moaned in a deep, breathy voice, and he ran on to his register. As her thoughts turned back to reality, she looked at me and said, "We share a locker together in the break room. Don't good-lookin' guys make your heart skip a beat?"

"Oh, my," I thought, "Here's my chance!" I quickly responded, "Well, actually, they used to. But praise God I found something better!"

"Something better?" she inquired anxiously. "What?"

"Men can only provide stagnant water. But Jesus gives me Living Water!" I replied.

Sensing her confusion and curiosity, I continued, "You can find out more about this Living Water in the Bible—check out the story of the Woman at the Well in the fourth chapter of John."

I wish I could say that our conversation went further, but tons of people waited behind me in line and I never saw that clerk again. Hopefully she went home and read that story. I have had to accept that all I can do sometimes is plant seeds and pray for laborers to come into her life to water them and help them grow.

Watching Seeds Sprout

However, once in while God blesses me with an extended window of opportunity, where I am privileged to not only pray and plant seeds, but I also get to watch them sprout into an amazing blossom as well. One day I was standing in the gymnasium at our church, watching my son play with some other children. One of the other moms approached me over in the corner and struck up a conversation. We chatted for some time and the subject came around to what stupid things we did as teenagers. I could tell this woman was fishing a little, so I decided to throw out some bait.

"I still struggle against doing stupid things, and I haven't been a teenager in over a decade!" I said.

The conversation continued superficially that day, but the next week, the woman knocked on my door and asked if our kids could play together while we talked. She said that she thought we might have a lot in common, and that she wanted us to spend some time getting to know each other. Eventually, I shared my personal testimony with her.

Soon afterward, she found the trust and courage to confide that her life was out of control. She reported daily Internet chat room activity, flying across the country to meet up with a chat room friend, and being unfaithful to her unsuspecting husband. We continued to meet for accountability, and she began seeing a counselor I recommended.

She had been abandoned by her father, and her mother had been an alcoholic since she could remember. She had suffered sexual abuse and had experimented with lesbianism. She was tired of living a double life, needing the adrenaline rush of feeling attractive and powerful one moment, then sinking into a pit of guilt and self-loathing the next.

Over the course of two years, I watched this woman break out of the chains that bound her—chains of unforgiveness and insecurity. She began to grasp the concepts of God's mercy and grace, and began walking with a new boldness and confidence in her step. She broke her generational curses and refused to hand down a legacy of abuse, neglect, alcoholism, and divorce to her children. She attended Bible study regularly and grew steadily in the knowledge of the Lord. She began teaching Bible studies later on, sharing the insights she had gained on her journey toward healing and wholeness. Her life became a living sacrifice—a sweet aroma pleasing to the Lord.

When you are blessed with the opportunity to witness God performing these miracles in women's lives, you can't help but rejoice with gladness. Witnessing the change God brings about in others through your testimony fuels your fire to continue to put aside your fear of what others may think of you and boldly go where few women have gone before—to the depths of truth. Don't be afraid to take off your mask. Don't be concerned about your image. Just be willing to be real with someone if you sense that truth is what she is looking for.

Fishing vs. Trespassing

Of course, know that there is a difference between throwing out a line to see if someone bites it and casting your pearls before swine. I don't go around advertising the fact that I am a recovering love addict. Boldness is good, but bluntness can turn people off. How do you know whether you are being inspired to be bold or tempted to be blunt? Examine your window of opportunity. Does an open window actually exist, or are you trying to throw a ball into a closed window and break the glass so that you can crawl through uninvited? You run a high risk of ripping your pants, cutting your flesh, or getting shot at by trying to climb through a broken window. If the window is closed, try gently rapping on it to see if you get a response. If not, then interceding in prayer on her behalf is all that you can do.

Let God orchestrate the opening of that window in His own time and in His own way. Is the window of opportunity only cracked a little, where you can toss in a short message and see if you get a response? Then throw a line and see if you get a bite. If not, be satisfied with planting a seed and pray that God sends other laborers to reap the harvest. If the window is wide open, and especially if the person is sticking her head out inviting you to come inside, then be bold, climb on through, and offer her a lifeline!

Never Take Your Eyes Off Yourself

As you go through life with your antenna up, scouting for other women who need this message, don't forget to always keep a check on your own thoughts and behaviors. If the devil can't make you bad, he'll make you busy! Satan will attempt to distract you from yourself and your own issues by making you busy ministering to others. He knows that if he can catch you off guard, he can discredit you as a witness and your message will be lost.

As long as you are glorifying God with your life and advancing His Kingdom by sharing your testimony, you will remain a walking target for Satan. I say this not to scare you, but simply so that you will be aware that constant vigilance needs to be exercised. Don't let your pride soften your defense. Thinking things like, "I'm strong enough now to go see that rated-R movie or to be alone with this person..." can quickly result in overwhelming temptation. A more sure defense consists of not allowing yourself to be put in those slippery places in the first place.

In her video, "No More Sheets," Juanita Bynum advises women to "stay as deep into the things of God as you once were into the things of the world," in order to avoid relapsing into old behaviors. As 1 Corinthians 10:12–13 says,

> *So, if you think you are standing firm, be careful that you don't fall! No temptation has seized you except what is common to [woman]. And God is faithful; He will not let you be tempted beyond what you can bear. But when you are tempted, He will also provide a way out so that you can stand up under it.*

If you want to stand up under any temptation, don't hesitate to take the escape route that God promises to provide!

Before we end our journey together toward sexual integrity (not that we have arrived, but that it is time to spread our own wings and fly from this nest with God's wind beneath our wings), I'd like to share a few encouraging words for women in various stages of life—singleness, courtship, marriage, and motherhood.

Final Words of Wisdom for Single Women

If you are single, the greatest admonition I can possibly give to you is to savor this season of your life, not wasting a single moment worrying about what your future holds. Don't wait for an earthly relationship to come along before you begin to pursue personal goals and do what you enjoy.

Take advantage of this time to finish your degree, take continuing education courses, or teach a class. Take art lessons, learn to play guitar, or plant a garden. Set aside some money to invest, and begin saving for your future. Go to the zoo by yourself, and take time to actually read about the animals. Learn to rollerblade, or take a kick-boxing class. Invite a female friend to walk and talk with you. Adopt a little sister, or spend time volunteering at your local nursing home or hospital. Find a place to plug in at your church—the choir, the youth group, or teaching Sunday school. Take a loaf of bread to the park to feed the ducks. Set the table for two with your nicest place settings, a candle, and wildflowers and invite Jesus to be a guest at your dinner table. Treat yourself and enjoy everything life has to offer.

Most importantly, seek to know God more intimately in these days, for only He knows what your future holds and what you can be doing even now to prepare for it. Remember that one of the most important things you can do is choose to be happy now! I believe that happiness is a choice, and if you can't choose to be happy as a single person, you'll never be happy married, either. Can't think of a reason to be happy? Look at your salvation! Your Savior has given you His unconditional love and forgiveness. He has given you a new heart, a new mind, and a new life. Now give Him your unconditional trust and live in such a way that you bring Him glory and delight.

Continue to make your love relationship with Him priority number one. Meditate daily on Matthew 6:33, "But seek first His kingdom and His righteousness, and all these things will be given to you as well. Therefore do not worry about tomorrow, for tomorrow will worry about itself." Each day is a gift to you from God. That is why it is called the "present." What you do with each day is your gift back to God.

Final Words of Wisdom for Courting Women

For those of you who are (or who will someday be) involved in a relationship, the best advice I can give is that *time is your friend!* As Women at the Well, we've never been known for our enduring patience in relationships, but be aware that there is nothing worse than rushing into a marriage only to find out that he isn't who you thought he was! And marrying him before he knows who you really are (mood swings, bad hair days, and all) isn't fair, either.

You may be excited to have an intimate relationship in your life once again, but it's easy for strangers to be intimate. Every detail the two of you share will be new and intriguing. But will the intimacy continue after you are no longer strangers? Can you still be intimate friends? Can you be satisfied with being intimate friends for a long period of time before becoming intimate lovers, or are your hormones dragging you through the friendship stage too quickly to discern whether or not you even like this person?

Over the past thirteen years of marriage, my husband and I have witnessed several couples meet, date, and marry within a few months' time. We've also seen the majority of those marriages disintegrate within the first few years. Those that begin with a "bang" usually either end with a bang or fizzle out quickly.

Courting relationships need to withstand the test of time, so that you can experience some of life's normal ups and downs together. Fair-weather friends are easy to find, but your husband needs to be a steady friend through thick and thin. Anyone can appear to be Mr. Right for a few months. Most guys can be charming and romantic at the beginning of any relationship. But what about when the new wears off? Will his true colors still be as vibrant? Will he still be as exciting to you and as excited about you? Will he still treat you with dignity and respect? Will he (and you) depend on God and trust in God's timing in the progression of your relationship, or will the two of you rush to the altar out of fear that you might lose the "best thing that ever happened to you"? Only time can answer that question. Only time can reveal the true godliness of his character. An ungodly husband will destroy your self-esteem and may eventually use your past against you, but a godly husband can minister to you throughout life like no one else can.

As you are investing this time in the relationship, don't make the mistake of putting your relationship with God in the back seat. Remember that anything treasured above God will eventually disappoint you. Continue investing the majority of your time and effort in your relationship with God, and see if your partner is doing the same thing. Two people relating intimately with God for the long haul will find it much easier to relate intimately with one another for the long haul.

Final Words of Wisdom for Married Women

Proverbs 4:23 says, "Above all else, guard your heart..." and I'd like to add, "Above all earthly relationships, guard your marriage!" Remember those parts of your wedding vows that said, "Leaving your family, cleaving to your husband, forsaking all others," etc., etc.? Take that part seriously. Don't allow any outside family member or friendship jeopardize your total commitment to your husband.

Your spouse is the one earthly relationship that will provide the majority of your joy (or the majority of your misery!) in life. You spend approximately twenty years living with your parents. You'll spend approximately twenty years living with your children. But hopefully you will live with your husband "until death do you part." You must treasure this person and cherish him above any other relationship. You must invest time building one another up, bonding together, and safeguarding the relationship from outside interferences.

As I have mentioned before, remember that people get married, not buried. As long as you are breathing, you will at times experience temptation outside of marriage. That ring on your finger does not exempt you from being human. And the marriage vows you took are not enough to keep you from falling into the pit that Satan has masterfully dug and camouflaged. With over fifty percent of couples eventually divorcing, people have been falling into that pit for generations and tossing their wedding vows out the window in the process.

Many of these divorces are a result of marital unfaithfulness, because sexuality is the one area where Satan has been most actively distorting people's minds since the dawn of creation. In fact, Satan distorts sexuality seven different ways in the Book of Genesis (polygamy, 4:19; homosexuality, 19:5; fornication and rape, 34:2; prostitution, 38:13–15; incest, 38:16–18; evil seduction, 39:7). With Satan coloring our image of sexuality so blatantly, it is easy to forget that sex is something God created and gave to humans as a perfect gift, prior to the fall of man, to be enjoyed only within marriage.

Even though your mind and body may have been defiled prior to marriage by unholy sexual acts, that doesn't necessarily guarantee that your marriage bed will be defiled also. To say that sex would continue to be a shameful, dirty act would also be saying that we are still shameful and dirty women. But because of what Christ did for us on the cross, we can know without a doubt that we are no longer the woman we once were. Therefore, sex will no longer be the "tool" or the "drug" for us that it once was. No, sex can be as exquisitely beautiful, as completely bonding, and as intensely pleasurable as God designed it to be.

In his book, *The Mystery of Marriage: As Iron Sharpens Iron,* Mike Mason gives this vivid illustration of how incredible God intended sex within marriage to be:

> What moment in a man's life can compare with that of the wedding night, when a beautiful woman takes off all her clothes and lies next to him in bed, and that woman is his wife? What can

equal the surprise of finding out that the one thing above all others which mankind has been most enterprising and proficient in dragging through the dirt turns out in fact to be the most innocent thing in the world? Is there any other activity at all which an adult man and woman may engage in together (apart from worship) that is actually more childlike, more clean and pure, more natural and wholesome and unequivocally right than is the act of making love? For if worship is the deepest available form of communion with God (and especially that particular act of worship known as Communion), then surely sex is the deepest communion that is possible between human beings, and as such is something absolutely essential (in more than a biological way) to our survival.[1]

Final Words of Wisdom for Mothers

If (or when) you have children, know what an incredible miracle from God they are and how much confidence God must have had in you, in order to place them into your care. Regardless of your past, God obviously knows that you can rise above those things and be an incredible asset to your children's formative years. You must be the woman that breaks this generational curse in your family and passes on a healthy heritage to your sons and daughters. You must teach your children, by example, what it means to be an overcomer. Show them what it means to be a new creation. Exercise and seek out forgiveness. Walk in humble obedience. Live a life of worship. Teach your children that true fulfillment comes only from God, not from human relationships.

Proverbs 22:6 says, "Train a child in the way he should go, and when he is old he will not turn from it." If you want to be a godly parent, you must be countercultural in your parenting. You will, of course, want to teach your daughters modesty and propriety. You will also want to teach your sons how to respect and honor women. And if you are concerned about preventing sex and/or love addiction in your children (as we all are), here are a few practical things that you can do to provide for your children's physical and emotional needs:

1. Invest in and maintain a healthy marriage. Your child's image of marriage will come directly from your marriage relationship. Make sure you are giving a healthy image. Your child's security as an individual is a direct reflection of his or her sense of security in the family unit.

2. Provide for your children's need for physical touch. Never stop hugging them, regardless of how old or how tall they become. Snuggle together on the couch while watching a family movie. Play-wrestle with them on the floor. Give them massages. Tickle them incessantly. Pat them on the back often.

3. Kiss your children often and spontaneously. Use affection as a genuine expression, not just as a hello or a goodbye.

4. Tell them you love them frequently, and be creative in how you do it. Tell them specifically what you love about them. Pick them flowers. Tuck a sweet note in their backpack. Mail them a special card. Surprise them by showing up at school for lunch.

5. Spend time doing what they enjoy doing. Participate in their favorite hobbies. Play soccer in the back yard. Make an art project with them. Take them swimming. Invite them on a walk. Let them help you cook. (Then let them help you clean up!)

6. Spend some time each day talking face-to-face without distractions. Tucking them in at bedtime is a great way to relax and focus on whatever it is that they want to talk about.

7. Regular family devotions foster intimacy with God as well as increase conversation and intimacy between family members. Bible stories and daily prayer time is vital.

8. Provide appropriate sex education at each age level. If we don't teach our children God's sexual values, the world will teach them its values! Being the first person to explain the truths about God's perfect design for sexuality will make *you* the expert in their minds, not the kids at school.

9. Make time to be alone with each child regularly and express consistently that they can ask you or tell you anything. Our children each get a "Mommy date" or a "Daddy date" regularly for such special conversations. Now, when our kids need to talk about something privately, they ask us if we will take them on a date!

10. Make time for yourself. If you need a short break for the sake of your sanity, put yourself in "time out" for a few minutes. Give the kids an activity to keep them busy, or ask a friend to fill in for thirty minutes. Read Scripture or a chapter in your favorite book. Take a bubble bath. Do some stretching exercises. Learn to de-stress rather than destruct. Don't feel guilty for needing some time of your own. Your spouse and your children will benefit.

Where Do We Go From Here?

My final prayer is that you truly have received an awakening by the Holy Spirit through these pages, and that you will continue to invest in your new heavenly affair. I ask that your prayers include the other parched women still looking for the Living Water that you have discovered. Out of your newfound intimacy, satisfaction, and devotion, won't you lead other Women at the Well to Jesus, too?

Here's one last word of wisdom especially for you, from T.D. Jakes' *The Lady, Her Lover, and Her Lord*:

Although your past may be laced with tragedy and filled with pain, God still offers the balm that heals. He erases the scarred and bleeding residue that attests to the horrors you have incurred. He is there to show you how to maximize on the maladies of yesterday. Take those traumas and tragedies, and turn them around. No matter what you have been through, remember you're still here. You're a survivor, and some little girl needs to know your recipe for survival. She doesn't need to hear about your successes; she needs to hear about your failures. Somewhere in the streets, there is someone dying because they do not know that it is possible to live through what you have already endured. You are a precious commodity. You are the cure to the crises. I know you say, "How can I be the cure when I myself am hurting?" Look at Jesus. He was giving life when He was dying. He healed the pained because of His pain. He was wounded for our transgressions. Could it be that you went through all you have so that you could help someone else?[2]

Richest blessings to you, my sister in Christ. And richest blessings to those that you touch with these *Words of Wisdom for Women at the Well.*

 QUESTIONS FOR
INTROSPECTION:

• What have been the greatest revelations the Lord has given you through these twelve chapters?

- Where would you be without those revelations?

- Are you willing to share those revelations with another woman who is still in the dark? Why or why not?

- Could pride keep you from sharing your personal testimony with someone who needed it? Why or why not?

- What did the neon sign on your forehead used to say?

- What does the neon sign on your forehead say now?

- Have you begun to notice neon signs on other women's foreheads?

- Are there particular women you can think of that need to know how to find the Living Water you have discovered?

- How, specifically, can you find an opportunity to throw out a line to see if she bites?

- How, specifically, can you keep your own love affair with the Lord alive while ministering to other women?

- On a separate sheet of paper, write a love letter to Jesus expressing your appreciation for all that He has done in your life.

Endnotes

CHAPTER 2

1 Dr. Harry Schaumburg, *False Intimacy* (Colorado Springs, CO: Navpress, 1992), 54.

2 T.D. Jakes, *The Lady, Her Lover, and Her Lord* (New York, NY: Putnam Publishers, 1998), 124–125.

CHAPTER 4

1 Schaumburg, *False Intimacy*, 60.

2 Steve Sampson, *I Was Always On My Mind* (Tonbridge, Kent [England]: Sovereign World Ltd., 1996), 20.

CHAPTER 6

1 Schaumburg, *False Intimacy*, 75.

CHAPTER 7

1 Gary R. Collins, Ph.D., *Biblical Basis of Christian Counseling for People Helpers* (Colorado Springs, CO: Navpress, 1993), 153.

2 Jakes, *The Lady, Her Lover, and Her Lord*, 16.

3 *Ibid.*, 19.

CHAPTER 8

[1] Daniel Green and Mel Lawrenz, *Why Do I Feel Like Hiding?* (Grand Rapids, MI.: Baker Books, 1994), 113.

[2] Robin Norwood, *Daily Meditations for Women Who Love Too Much* (New York, NY: Putnam Publishers, 1997), May 22.

[3] Collins, *Biblical Basis of Christian Counseling for People Helpers*, 113.

CHAPTER 9

[1] Charles R. Solomon,, *Handbook to Happiness* (Wheaton, IL: Tyndale House, 1989), 42–43.

[2] *Ibid.*, 44–45.

[3] Robert S. McGee, *Father Hunger* (Ann Arbor, MI: Servant, 1993), 213–214.

[4] *Ibid.*, 215.

CHAPTER 10

[1] Beth J. Leuders, *Aspire Magazine* (June/July 1998), 39.

[2] Joshua Harris, *I Kissed Dating Goodbye*, (Sisters, OR: Multnomah, 1997), 141.

[3] Elisabeth Elliot, *Passion & Purity*, (Grand Rapids, MI: Revel, 1984), 99.

CHAPTER 11

[1] Collins, *Biblical Basis of Christian Counseling for People Helpers*, 237.

CHAPTER 12

[1] Mike Mason, *The Mystery of Marriage* (Portland, OR: Multnomah Press, 1985), 121.

[2] Jakes, *The Lady, Her Lover, and Her Lord*, 42–43.

Would you like to start a
Women at the Well growth group
in your local church, college campus,
or neighborhood?

CONTACT US TO ORDER A COPY OF

Words of Wisdom for Well Women
40 Devotions of Preparation
for Leading Women at the Well
to Living Water

For more information about Well Women Ministries, other resources by Shannon Ethridge, or to schedule speaking engagements, please contact:

Shannon Ethridge
Well Women Ministries
P.O. Box 1018, Lindale, TX 75771
shannonethridge@everywomansbattle.com
1-800-NEW LIFE
www.everywomansbattle.com

Printed in the United States
114610LV00002B/127/A

9 781553 066781